United States of America

MEXICO

GUADALAJARA ✗

MEXICO CITY

MERIDA ✗

✗ VALLADOLID

Campeche

PUERTO VALLARTA ✗

✗

Chinantlan Mountains

✗

TULUM

CHOLULA ↕ PUEBLA ✗

✗

YUCATAN

RICK STEIN
The Road to
MEXICO

BBC BOOKS

This book is dedicated to Ed, Jack and Charlie and Sas, Zach and Olive

10 9 8 7 6 5 4 3 2 1

BBC Books, an imprint of Ebury Publishing
20 Vauxhall Bridge Road, London SW1V 2SA

BBC Books is part of the Penguin Random House
group of companies whose addresses can be found
at global.penguinrandomhouse.com

First published by BBC Books in 2017
www.eburypublishing.co.uk

A CIP catalogue record for this book
is available from the British Library

ISBN 9781785942006

Printed and bound in Italy by L.E.G.O. S.p.A

Penguin Random House is committed to a
sustainable future for our business, our readers
and our planet. This book is made from Forest
Stewardship Council® certified paper.

Penguin Random House UK

This book is published to accompany the television
series entitled *Rick Stein: The Road to Mexico*
first broadcast on BBC Two in 2017. *Rick Stein:
The Road to Mexico* is a Denhams production.

Producers: David Pritchard & Arezoo Farahzad
Executive producer for Denhams: Grace Kitto
Executive producer for the BBC: David Brindley

MIX
Paper from
responsible sources
FSC® C018179

Commissioning editor: Lizzy Gray
Editor: Charlotte Macdonald
Project editor: Jinny Johnson
Design and art direction: Smith & Gilmour
Photographer: James Murphy
Home economist: Portia Spooner
Food stylist: Aya Nishimura
Prop stylist: Penny Markham
Illustrator: Andy Smith

I first went to Mexico in 1968. I crossed the border from the USA at Nuevo Laredo and headed for the city of Monterrey. That night in a taquería I ordered some tacos. I didn't know what they were; I just pointed to some locals eating them and asked to have the same. The tacos were filled with some cooked meat, I think it was pork, and came with chopped tomatoes, onions, green peppers, which were in fact chillies, and a herb I later realised was coriander. There were slices of lime alongside and a bowl of orange-red sauce. It's no exaggeration to say that this meal changed my life. My memory is of the sourness of the lime, the freshness and heat of the salad and the red salsa, a comforting mouthful of salty, spicy pork and the warm alkaline smell and taste of corn tortillas. I had never tasted anything so vivid, so demanding, so exciting. It was like listening to Little Richard's 'Tutti Frutti' for the first time, so loud and immediate, a brief and delicious assault on the senses, leaving you wanting more.

The next morning, after a night in a really rough hotel, I took a bus to the outskirts of town and started to walk, looking to hitch a ride to Ciudad Victoria and Tampico. It was early and cold but sunny, with a smell of just-lit charcoal in the air. I went into a little breakfast place where I could see people eating and again pointed to a plate of food. This time it was fried eggs with tortillas under them and the same sort of hot red sauce as I'd had the night before poured over the top. I ordered coffee, which came without milk. I was too nervous to ask for any, and there and then my abiding love of Mexican breakfasts began with this dish – huevos rancheros. I've eaten it many times since and I always insist on café negro to go with it.

I had arrived for the first time in New York on a German cargo ship, having spent two years journeying around Australia and New Zealand. Most of the time I was travelling alone. It was part of an extended and unplanned round-the-world trip I went on after my father died. I bought a 99-dollar ticket for 99 days unlimited travel on Greyhound buses and did the eastern seaboard all the way to Florida. Some nights to save money, I took the bus on a long trip so I could sleep overnight, then partly retraced my steps the next morning. After Florida I did Mardi Gras in New Orleans and headed to Houston. Everywhere was cold. Even in Texas I was cold, tired and lonely. I had a book of D. H. Lawrence essays with me at the time: *Mornings in Mexico*. They painted a world which seemed exotic, warm and romantic, almost like some part of the Mediterranean: '*There – is a resinous smell of ocote wood, and a smell of coffee, and a faint smell of leaves, and of morning, Mexico has a faint, physical scent of her own, as each human being has. And this is a curious, inexplicable scent, in which there are resin and perspiration and sunburned earth.*' Reading words like these, no wonder I wanted to go to Mexico.

I spent a couple of months travelling through the country, going to Tampico, Ciudad Valles, Mexico City, Acapulco, Taxco, Guadalajara, Mazatlán, and my love of the food of Mexico was born.

Later, I resolved to give the States another try. I had met lots of Californians in Acapulco and they seemed different to the people I'd encountered on the buses in the East. They were more like Australians, though they were all constantly smoking marijuana, which shocked me at the time. I went to San Francisco, visited Fisherman's Wharf, ate vegetarian food in Haight Ashbury, went to a party at a farm down a dirt road in an orange grove, with the scent of blossom in the night air. I listened to The Doors, to Jefferson Airplane, to the Mamas and the Papas, and the reality of 'California Dreaming' as a place of warmth and sunshine, an escape from winter and grey skies, came home to me.

That was my experience of California back then. What would it be like today?

I planned the trip for this book and TV series as a retracing of my journey nearly fifty years ago. Would the California I remembered be as exciting now? I've been back to Mexico a few times since then, filming in northern Mexico, Chihuahua and Zacatecas, and for holidays with Sas, my wife, on the Pacific coast in Oaxaca, and in Yucatán and Mexico City. It's a country we've both fallen in love with – the people, the bright colours, the dazzling markets, the music, the sense of an ancient land filled with volcanoes and Aztec, Zapotec and Mayan temples, the churches and cathedrals, and the troubled and violent history, which is most arrestingly summed up in the gigantic murals of Rivera, Orozco and Siqueiros. And above all it's the food that brings us back.

But since then, the awful stories of corruption have become all too familiar. How would I get on in a Mexico with a daily tragedy of death from the activities of the drug traffickers, the narcos? Would California be a place gone crazy with food allergies and political correctness about food? Someone joked to me the other day that you could probably hold up a bank in California armed with a loaf of factory bread, so petrified everyone seems to be about gluten. I should have known better about both places. Within a couple of hours of landing in Mexico City I had smelt hot corn tacos, an aroma as evocative to me as when in my twenties I got off the ferry in Boulogne and caught the smell of Gauloises and highly roasted coffee. I had also read something quite reassuring on a US website saying that as a tourist, you're more likely to die an unnatural death in Australia than in Mexico. In other words, I was entering a country safe for tourists, and while I am appalled by the loss of life from the drugs trade, I felt it shouldn't stop me from going back to a land filled with lovely, engaging, warm-hearted people whose enthusiasm for their cuisine is immense.

It's a strange thing, maybe down to journalists and their need to make something out of nothing, but I generally find that when things are reported to be going wrong they're often not as bad as they seem. There was indeed in California a widespread understanding of gluten intolerance and other food allergies everywhere I went, but the knowledge and helpfulness in any food outlet was very apparent. I suddenly began to realise that the rather crusty view of the over-exaggeration of allergens actually misses the point that sadly many people do suffer from allergies. In California they've taken this on board.

Also, something I've often thought about the States is that what happens there tends to end up coming here. This is normally things like unhealthy fast food or chewing gum on pavements but applies to good stuff, too. On the first day in San Francisco, I went to the Ferry Building Market and entered a world of grown-up produce. The Cowgirl Creamery's Artisan Cheese Shop, Far West Funghi, Farm Fresh to You, The Golden Gate Meat Company and The Hog Island Oyster Company – these names alone painted an attractive picture of thoughtful local food. Indeed, they've invented a word for people who make a decision only to buy local, be it food and drink or indeed any other product, 'locavore'. Local was the mantra of the Cowgirl Creamery, who describe one of their cheeses, Mt Tam, with this clever tasting note 'cultured butter with hints of white mushroom'. The Hog Island Oyster people talk about Tomales Bay, the location of their oyster beds, in irresistible language, 'the cool, clean water rich in plankton that oysters feed on to grow plump and sweet, and the flavor of the bay is evident in every delicious mouthful'. At the market there were wonderful Cabernets and Chardonnays from the Napa Valley, of course; a stall devoted to more kinds of wild mushroom than you'd see even in a French market; sourdough bread and comfortable cafés selling open sourdough sandwiches piled high with prosciutto and the first tomatoes of the season. Outside was a farmers' market showcasing the new season's garlic and the first punnets of strawberries.

Years ago I made a series in Britain and Ireland called *Food Heroes* in which we went everywhere looking for growers and producers of excellent food. We found plenty but no one had much clue about how to sell their produce. In California they've understood how to involve producers with customers for many years. It goes right back to the early days of restaurants like Chez Panisse in Berkeley, where Alice Waters and the head chef Jeremiah Tower decided one day to scrap the hitherto French-influenced bistro menu and just do a few starters, mains and sweets based entirely on what they could buy locally. It seems such an obvious decision now but not so at the time, and from that and a few like-minded people a new attitude to food was formed, and it is something that still governs what most of us involved with food believe to this day.

On this new journey, I travelled with the TV crew all the way from San Francisco to Tijuana, they in a minibus, me in a pale blue convertible Ford Mustang, which was heaven. I drove out to Hog Island to have some oysters and to Berkeley for lunch at Chez Panisse. Leaving San Francisco, I drove down the Salinas Valley, marvelling at the overwhelming scale of agricultural production there, and on to Monterey and Cannery Row. I ate sand soles at a restaurant called The Sardine Factory and remembered how important food is in John Steinbeck's lyrical book. Then on to Pismo Beach, where I walked along by the ocean and ordered a California clam chowder poured into a scooped-out sourdough roll. I ate pixie tangerines and avocados straight off the trees at Ojai near Santa Barbara. I stopped off at the Hitching Post where I had a large steak cooked over a California oak grill and drank the same Pinot as Paul Giamatti did in the film *Sideways*. Then I gunned down Pacific Highway 1 to Santa Monica listening to The Beach Boys and to Lana del Ray's 'Summertime Sadness'. In LA I had to have a bowl of chilli in Barney's Beanery and talk to the locals about Jim Morrison and Janice Joplin, both regulars. 'Which was Jim's seat?' I asked at the bar. 'All of them' was the answer. In San Diego, I just had to go to a local diner called Rudfords and eat steak and eggs for breakfast. Everywhere I went no one talked politics; everyone talked about food. There's an awful lot to love about California.

I've called this book *The Road to Mexico* because, in addition to remembering my first trip to California and the cooking there, I have begun to realise that there is so much Mexican influence in Californian food. It's extraordinary how popular Mexican is becoming everywhere, and the first impressions I had all those years ago are still the same. Basically it's about the extraordinary combination of savoury, spicy, fresh and sour. When people say that Mexican food is all the same, it's all tacos, they miss the point. Tortillas (tacos are filled tortillas) are to Mexican cuisine what pasta is to Italian. They are the framework on which Mexican cooks build incredibly sophisticated variations of flavours and textures.

Another enjoyable outcome of the Mexican culinary influence in Los Angeles is the way that the cooking of other ethnic minorities is mixed with Mexican. I'd heard of Indian-Mexican, like chicken tikka masala quesadillas, but there's also Korean-Mexican. We filmed at Kogi, a famous food truck just across the road from the HBO headquarters in Hollywood. Kogi specialises in tacos with kimchi. The slow-cooked pork filling is Mexican but the additions are the highly spiced Korean fermented cabbage, kimchi, and a Korean red chilli paste, Gochujang, which you can now buy in some supermarkets here. I had a spirited conversation with Roy Choi, the owner, and it became clear to me that what I thought of as an outrageous Californian appropriation of other people's ideas was in fact a perfectly normal and unselfconscious mix of great flavours.

People think that Mexican food is quite heavy and indeed it can be. You might have a pile of warm tortillas, a tray full of hot slow-cooked beef brisket, barbacoa, flavoured with chipotle chilli, garlic, oregano and cider vinegar, served maybe with avocado, soured cream, a couple of salsas, raw onions and coriander to add, but you make of it what you will. You can help yourself to one taco or ten. The tortilla is sometimes little more than a way of picking up food, and I've had some of the lightest most refreshing dishes with the tortilla as a base – often seafood like raw tuna with guacamole, tomato and shallots; crab with a little mayonnaise, green jalapeño chillies, cherry tomatoes and lime; courgette flowers with serrano chillies and spring onions cooked on la plancha with a cheese like mozzarella called Oaxacan cheese. There's a delightful chicken soup called sopa Azteca containing thin strips of tortilla spiced with chillies and enriched with little cubes of avocado. I ate fish simply split open like a kipper and grilled and served with green and red salsas; you can pick up the fish with tortillas or just eat it on its own. Leaving savoury things, there are the most beautiful concoctions of tropical fruit sprinkled with chilli and lime, and finally Mexico has some of the most delightful fresh fruit drinks known to man. The variety is endless.

I hope you can gather that like so many who visit Mexico I am besotted with the food. This isn't a book for purists, though. I often feel I've only scratched the surface. I haven't really attempted to explain the enormous importance of certain dishes like pozole or chiles en nogada at festival times, not to mention tamales on *Día de los Muertos* (Day of the Dead). I've taken a few liberties, simplified the mole poblano, used chipotles rather than pasillas in my sopa Azteca, generally suggested buying in tortillas rather than making your own and aimed to make things as easy as possible for you to make here. But I have tried to explain why Mexican food works for me and why I think it is one of the world's greatest cuisines.

GUAJILLO

MULATO

CHIPOTLE
MORITA'

ARBOL

PASILLA

ANCHO

HABANERO

JALAPEÑO

POBLANO

SERRANO

DESAYUNOS y ALMUERZOS

BREAKFAST & BRUNCH

Somerset Maugham once said, 'To eat well in England you should have breakfast three times a day.' Happily this is no longer true in the UK and perhaps never was in Mexico, but there is an element of truth when it comes to Mexican restaurants; for me, breakfast there has always been the best meal of the day. Never are warm tortillas, chilli salsa and cups of steaming coffee more welcome. It's also the time to see a pleasant slice of Mexican life, as families, large families, sit down together for breakfast in restaurants all over Mexico. I don't know if I always get a bit excited after my first cup of coffee in the morning, but I recall telling the crew on three or four occasions that we should be filming breakfast time. This was particularly the case at the Hostería del Marqués in Valladolid, and I've written about the huevos motuleños we ate there on page 35 . I could equally have waxed lyrical about the food at the hotel we stayed in at Oaxaca, La Catrina de Alcalá. Every morning they serve the usual dishes like huevos rancheros and divorciados, but they also do omelettes stuffed with the freshest and most tender local vegetables. One morning it was coriander and spinach; on another tiny green peas, chard and spring onions. I must confess the breakfast recipe on page 39, crab and avocado omelette, is my Padstow seafood take on those lovely omelettes.

Incidentally, no one should turn down an opportunity to go to Oaxaca. It's a beautiful small city and many say it has the best cooking in Mexico. There's also a spiritually uplifting archaeological site there called Monte Albán, built by the Zapotec on a hilltop above the city. It's a city of beautiful churches, including my favourite in Mexico, Santo Domingo. An artist friend of mine, Phil Kelly, painted it many times. Sadly Phil died a few years ago but I have a number of his paintings of Mexico in my restaurants. They are intensely energetic, colourful and slightly out of control as was Phil – as is Mexico.

The early morning restaurants in cities like Guadalajara and Mexico City are all about noise and bustle. When you walk into Fonda Margarita in Mexico City at 7am you're confronted by about a dozen giant terracotta pots bubbling away over charcoal. There might be a pork stew with tomatillos in one, deep-fried pig skin (*chicharrón*) in a chilli and tomato salsa in another, but the least daunting dish to order for breakfast is refried beans with scrambled eggs, and you'll find my version on page 27.

RANCH-STYLE EGGS & DIVORCED EGGS

These excellent breakfast dishes are quite similar. Indeed the only difference is that divorciados includes both a green sauce and a red sauce. It starts with two fried eggs, each on a tortilla with salsa verde sauce on one and salsa ranchero on the other. The point is that the sauces are separated – divorced – by simply spacing them on the plate or by putting a line of refried beans between them. Huevos rancheros should have just salsa ranchero, though being Mexico there might be salsa verde as well! Rancheros is a nostalgic dish for me because when I first went to Mexico in the 60s it's what I had every day for breakfast, always with a cup of black coffee and no milk. Chilli and black coffee in the morning – perfection.

SERVES FOUR

8 x 15cm *Corn tortillas*
   (page 44 or bought)
oil, for frying
4–8 eggs (1 or 2 per person)
250g *Refried beans*
   (page 104), warmed
60g Lancashire or feta
   cheese, crumbled
1 tbsp chopped coriander

For the salsa ranchero
1 medium onion
4 cloves garlic
2 green serrano or
   jalapeño chillies,
   stems removed, halved
½ tsp ground cumin
400g tin plum tomatoes
½ tsp salt
2 tbsp corn oil

SERVES TWO

4 x 15cm *Corn tortillas*
   (page 44 or bought)
oil, for frying
4 eggs
6 tbsp *Stewed salsa verde*
   (page 295), warmed
6 tbsp *Salsa ranchero*
   (above), warmed
4 tbsp *Refried beans*
   (page 104), warmed
1 tbsp chopped fresh
   coriander
40g Lancashire cheese,
   crumbled (optional)
Salt and pepper

HUEVOS RANCHEROS

For the salsa, put the onion, garlic, chillies, cumin, tomatoes and salt in a blender and blitz to a smooth sauce. Heat the corn oil in a saucepan, then pour in the contents of the blender. Simmer for about 10 minutes, check seasoning and add a little more salt if required, then keep the sauce warm.

Warm the tortillas in a dry frying pan, in a microwave or in the oven (page 306). In a separate frying pan, heat some oil and fry the eggs. Place 2 overlapping corn tortillas on each plate, top them with refried beans, some of the ranchero sauce and fried eggs. Add a scattering of crumbled cheese and chopped coriander, then serve immediately.

HUEVOS DIVORCIADOS

Warm the tortillas in a dry frying pan, in a microwave or in the oven (page 306). In a separate frying pan, heat some oil and fry the eggs.

While the eggs are cooking, put 2 overlapping tortillas on each plate. Add 3 spoonfuls of stewed salsa verde and 3 spoonfuls of salsa ranchero on each, with a 'wall' of 2 tablespoons of refried beans between them. Put a fried egg on each pool of salsa. Sprinkle with chopped coriander and crumbled cheese, if using, then season with salt and pepper and serve. *Recipe photograph overleaf*

FRIED TORTILLA CHIPS IN GREEN SALSA WITH CRUMBLED CHEESE

I doubt whether you would ever find a breakfast buffet in Mexico that didn't contain chilaquiles. The reason is quite simple. They're a perfect way of using up stale tortillas, which are cut into triangles, then fried or baked and known as totopos. Basic chilaquiles are then simmered with either salsa verde or salsa roja until they start to soften, but it's important to serve them while still partly crisp. This recipe is for the green-sauce version, with a fried egg, some crumbled cheese and a little soured cream and chopped coriander.

It would be normal and scrumptious to add a spoonful or two of refried beans as well.

SERVES FOUR

¼ onion, chopped
1½ green serrano or
   jalapeño chillies,
   stems removed, halved
2 cloves garlic, chopped
125ml *Chicken stock*
   (page 300) or water
380g tin tomatillos
2 tbsp corn oil
½ tsp salt
300ml corn or vegetable
   oil, for frying
12 x 15cm *Corn tortillas*
   (page 44 or bought),
   each cut into 8 wedges
4 eggs
75g Lancashire or feta
   cheese, crumbled
1 shallot, finely sliced
1 tbsp roughly chopped
   coriander
4 tbsp soured cream

Put the onion, chillies, garlic, stock and tomatillos in a blender and blitz to make a sauce. Heat the 2 tablespoons of corn oil in a saucepan, add the sauce, then season to taste with salt and simmer for 5 minutes. Cook the sauce for longer if it's too watery to reduce it a little, or add more stock if it's too thick.

Next, heat the 300ml of oil to 190°C in a separate large pan. Fry the tortilla triangles until barely golden and crisp, then drain them on kitchen paper.

When the sauce is ready, fry the eggs. Stir the fried tortillas into the sauce, folding lightly to coat them but taking care not to break them up.

Divide the sauce and tortillas between 4 warm plates and top each one with a fried egg. Add crumbled cheese, sliced shallot, a sprinkle of coriander and some soured cream and serve immediately.

SCRAMBLED EGGS WITH REFRIED BEANS

Fondas are cheap neighbourhood restaurants that are open all hours, particularly for early breakfast. For me, this was the star dish at the Fonda Margarita restaurant in Mexico City. It's simply eggs scrambled with refried beans and formed into a large black lozenge shape. I make it more like an omelette, though, because it's easier to do. The combination of beans, lard and eggs is irresistible.

SERVES TWO

4 eggs
¼ tsp salt
10 turns black peppermill
10g lard
¼ quantity *Refried beans* (page 104)
Small handful coriander, chopped
1 avocado, stoned, peeled and sliced (optional)

Whisk the eggs with the salt and black pepper. Warm the lard in a non-stick frying pan, then pour in the eggs and move them gently around the pan as they start to scramble. Add the refried beans and leave the partly scrambled eggs to set on the bottom, then flip them over like an omelette.

Sprinkle with chopped coriander and serve with slices of avocado, if using.

SCRAMBLED EGGS WITH CHORIZO

Lalo! is a lively, highly coloured, informal restaurant in the Roma district of Mexico City, the trendiest part of town. Its owner is Eduardo García whose nickname is Lalo. He also owns the famous Maximo Bistrot just the other side of Zacatecas Street, which is much more upmarket. Both are full all the time. I met Lalo on a boating trip to the watery market garden area of Mexico City called Xochimilco and I liked him a lot. He and his family had a very hard life as migrant workers on farms all over the United States before he became a chef, and after his years out in the fields Lalo had no problem adapting to the demands of restaurant cooking. His food is Mexican, with a little European inspiration that reflects his years of working in French kitchens. It's modern but not trying to be clever and this is a perfect example.

SERVES FOUR

100g chorizo, crumbled
  or finely chopped
1 tbsp oil or butter
20g onion, finely chopped
20g green serrano or
  jalapeño chillies,
  very finely chopped
100g cooked potatoes,
  cut into 5mm dice
8 large eggs, beaten
30g Cotija cheese or
  Parmesan, grated
Small handful coriander,
  roughly chopped
1 ripe avocado, stoned,
  peeled and sliced
Sea salt
*Roasted red tomato
  and chilli salsa*
  (page 108), to serve

Heat a large dry frying pan and cook the chorizo briefly until it starts to give off some of its oil. Remove and set aside.

Heat the oil or butter in the frying pan. Add the onion and chillies and fry them over a high heat for 2 minutes, stirring all the time. Put the crumbled chorizo back in the pan, along with the diced potatoes, then cook for 2 more minutes. Add the beaten eggs and cook until softly set. Season with salt.

Sprinkle the eggs with grated cheese and chopped coriander and serve with some slices of avocado and roasted tomato salsa on the side.

GREEN JUICE

This bright green juice can be ordered in virtually any café or restaurant in Mexico. What it's actually going to be made of is always going to be different, depending on what fresh fruit and vegetables they've got in, but it will usually be made from a mixture of celery, nopales (part of the prickly pear plant), parsley and pineapple. It's wonderfully refreshing and normally slightly sweet and herbal tasting. Interestingly it solves the question I used to have of Mexican markets as to where all the fruit goes, because sweets or puddings in Mexican restaurants don't feature many fruit dishes. The answer is into jugo verde and perhaps a glorious concoction of chopped fruit with lime and chilli (page 261). *Recipe photograph overleaf*

SERVES TWO OR THREE

1 celery stick
150g fresh pineapple (about ¼ medium pineapple)
6cm piece of cucumber
Juice of 1 lime
Small handful parsley
I small green apple
Juice of 1 orange (about 150ml)

Peel, deseed and core the fruit and vegetables as necessary. Put it all in a blender or smoothie maker and blitz until smooth. Drink immediately, with ice, if desired.

FRIED EGGS ON TORTILLAS WITH TOMATO SALSA, HAM & PEAS

Previously, there was never any question that my favourite Mexican breakfast dish was huevos rancheros. But only on this journey did I discover huevos motuleños. It is a similar dish in that it has a chilli and tomato sauce, refried beans and tortillas, but the difference is that the tortillas are crisp and there's also queso fresco, chopped ham, peas and slices of creamy avocado. The best motuleños I had was at the Hostería del Marqués in Valladolid. As soon as you walk into the sunny central courtyard, alive with blossoms and surrounded by cool colonnades with colourful paintings and a long table piled high with watermelons, mangoes, pineapples, oranges and papayas, you know you're going to have a wonderful Mexican breakfast. It's worth pointing out that though the murals in the Palacio Municipal across the square are not up to Diego Rivera or Orozco standard, they are rather striking in a slightly disturbing way. There are the usual scenes of the Spanish murdering the local Mayans, and the locals are inevitably much nicer-looking people. *Recipe photograph overleaf*

SERVES FOUR
2 tsp lard or duck fat
Refried beans (page 104)
200ml corn or vegetable
  oil, for frying
4 x 12cm *Corn tortillas*
  (page 44 or bought)
4 eggs
75g Lancashire or feta
  cheese, crumbled
4 slices cooked ham,
  chopped or torn
1 avocado, stoned,
  peeled and sliced
Handful frozen peas, cooked
1 tbsp chopped coriander

For the tomato sauce
2–3 large ripe tomatoes,
  quartered
2 cloves garlic
1–2 red serrano or jalapeño
  chillies, stems removed,
  seeds in or out as you like
½ tsp dried oregano
2 tbsp oil
½ tsp salt

To make the tomato sauce, put the tomatoes, garlic, chillies and oregano in a blender with 125ml of water and process until smooth. Heat the oil in a pan, add the tomato mixture and cook for 5–6 minutes. Season with salt.

Heat the lard or duck fat and warm the refried beans, then set them aside. Heat the oil and fry the whole tortillas in batches for a minute or so on each side until crisp. Drain them on kitchen paper and keep them warm while you fry the eggs.

Put a crisp tortilla on each plate with some refried beans. Top with a fried egg, then add tomato sauce, crumbled cheese and ham. Top with a few slices of avocado and scatter with cooked peas and chopped coriander.

CRAB & AVOCADO OMELETTE WITH CHILLI & CORIANDER

Much as I love Mexican breakfasts like huevos divorciados or huevos motuleños, I've discovered they also do a super-simple, delicate omelette in Oaxaca. I recall a particularly delicious one, stuffed with courgette flowers, and though I have made this recipe up I'm sure I could find a crab omelette with avocado somewhere in Mexico.

Recipe photograph overleaf

SERVES TWO

6 eggs
¼ tsp salt
1 tsp grated Parmesan
   cheese
20g butter
80g crab meat (70g white
   mixed with 10g brown)
½ avocado, stoned,
   peeled and diced
½ green serrano or
   jalapeño chilli, finely
   sliced (seeds in)
1 tbsp coriander, chopped
2 spring onions, white
   part only, finely sliced
A few sprigs of coriander

Crack 3 of the eggs into a bowl and beat them lightly to break up the yolks. Season with a pinch of salt and half the Parmesan cheese.

Heat a 20cm non-stick frying pan, add half the butter and wait until it has melted and is sizzling. Add the eggs and let them bubble for a few seconds. Using a wooden spatula, gently draw in the sides, let the eggs set for 30–60 seconds, then repeat to mix the cooked egg with the uncooked egg.

Sprinkle half of the crab meat, avocado, spring onions, sliced chilli and coriander over half the surface of the omelette and let them heat through for up to a minute. The omelette should be soft and only semi-set (or 'baveuse' as they say in France).

With the spatula, flip the uncovered half of the omelette over the filling to form a half-moon shape. Slide it on to a serving plate and keep it warm while you make the second omelette in the same way. Serve immediately, sprinkled with a few sprigs of coriander.

TORTILLAS DE HARINA
FLOUR TORTILLAS

These are very much a staple of northern Mexican cuisine. Flavourwise, they don't match corn tortillas, but their advantage is that you can wrap food up in them easily, so they are very versatile.

MAKES 16 X 15CM TORTILLAS

450g plain flour, plus extra for dusting
1 tsp salt
1 tsp baking powder
80ml corn oil
250ml lukewarm water

In a food mixer fitted with a dough hook, mix the flour, salt and baking powder. Add the corn oil, then the water. Mix well for 2 minutes, stopping the machine and scraping down the mixture in the bowl when necessary. The mixture should start to come together in a ball. Knead it well for another minute or so.

Turn the dough out on to a floured board and divide into 16 pieces. Leave them to rest for 15–20 minutes.

Place a dry heavy-based frying pan over a fairly high heat. Using a rolling pin and a little more flour for dusting, roll out discs of about 15cm in diameter. Cook the tortillas in the hot pan, one at a time, for about a minute or until brown patches appear, then flip them over and cook on the other side for 30–40 seconds. Stack the tortillas in a tortilla basket with a lid if you have one, or on a warm plate covered with foil, to prevent them becoming dry and brittle.

Serve the tortillas warm with your choice of filling, or use them in burritos, quesadillas and so on.

CORN TORTILLAS

Good-quality, mass-produced corn tortillas have become much more readily available online since I started planning this book, and the need to make your own has diminished. I include a recipe because they are rewarding to make and taste the best, but I confess to buying them much more often. You still can't get proper corn tortillas in supermarkets, just the ones mixed with flour which don't taste right, but it won't be long.

MAKES 12 X 15CM TORTILLAS

250g maize tortilla flour (masa harina, or maseca)
½ tsp salt
350–375ml lukewarm water

Put the flour in a bowl with the salt. Add water, starting with 350ml. If the dough is still too dry to come together, add more water, a little at a time, until you have a soft but not sticky dough. Knead the dough for a minute or two until it is soft and pliable and forms a ball. Ideally, allow the dough to rest, covered, for 20–30 minutes for the best texture, but you can use it straight away if you need to.

Divide the mixture into golfball-sized balls. Place one between two sheets of thin polythene. Then press it in a tortilla press or roll with a rolling pin to make a disc about 15cm in diameter. Repeat to use the rest of the dough and pile the tortillas up, separated with baking parchment to prevent them sticking together.

Heat an ungreased heavy-based frying pan. Cook the tortillas, one or two at a time, until they change colour and start to puff up slightly; this will take about 2 minutes. Flip them over and repeat on the other side. Keep the tortillas warm (page 306).

You can make this dough in advance and store it, wrapped in cling film, in the fridge for a few days.

BLUE CORN TORTILLAS

MAKES 12 X 15CM TORTILLAS

250g blue corn tortilla flour (harina de maiz azul, or maseca azul)
275–300ml lukewarm water
½ tsp salt

The mixture for these is slightly different because of the absorbency of the flour. Make them as for white corn tortillas, but start by adding 275ml water, only adding more if the dough is too dry. Knead to a smooth, soft but not sticky dough. Keep the dough, very well wrapped, in the fridge until ready to use, then cook as for white corn tortillas.

ANTOJITOS Y GARNACHAS

STREETFOOD

maíz frito

Quite near the beach front in the Pacific resort of Puerto Vallarta there's a taco stand called Robles Birria Tacos. It's one of Puerto Vallarta's most popular breakfast places and it specialises in perhaps the most famous dish in the state of Jalisco – birria. This is a spicy stew traditionally made from goat or lamb, flavoured with guajillo and pasilla chillies, garlic, oregano, cumin and cider vinegar. The Robles family have run this stand since 1986 and Felipa, the mother, is there with her son and daughter every day. They begin serving at 8.30am and sometimes you have to wait 40 minutes in the queue to get your two or three tacos filled with meat, sliced onions, cucumber, coriander, radishes and either salsa verse or salsa roja and a squeeze of lime. Their birria tradition started on their family ranch 50 kilometres away and they brought it to a street stall in Puerto Vallarta; the birria takes seven hours to cook and it's heaven.

Their story is repeated all over Mexico. Streetfood is not about poor people selling cheap food to other poor people, it's an important and honourable tradition. Most taco stands will feature some sort of slow-cooked meat as the foundation and it's always about the contrast between the deep flavour of the meat and sharper tastes, like raw chillies, onions and radishes. The carnitas tacos on page 86 are a case in point, and although the restaurant where I ate them was in the Mission district of San Francisco, I could have been in Mexico City. You also find an amazing variety of parts of animals, including hearts, lungs, skin, tendons, penises, tails and eyeballs. Meat might be cooked in a pit in the ground, wrapped in agave leaves, or in lard, in trays of steam or slowly over charcoal. The recipe for birria is on page 244 in the meat chapter, as it's not just a streetfood taco but a Mexican lamb or goat stew that's served at home.

Tacos are the most popular item but many people think Mexico has the best and most varied streetfood in the world, be it corn on the cob with chilli and mayo, mackerel in batter with chilli and lime, hot tamales, empanadas, chicken enchiladas or slow-cooked pork with achiote. The Mexicans call the food prepared by street vendors *antojitos* – little cravings. I crave a return to Mexico for them every day.

BLUE CORN & CHEESE QUESADILLAS WITH COURGETTE FLOWERS

These tortilla turnovers filled with cheese come from Xochimilco market, 20 miles or so from the centre of Mexico City. Pronounced 'Sochimilco', the market is right next to an area of wetlands that contains artificial islands called *chinampas*, where all the vegetables in the market will have been grown. The quesadillas were made from blue corn and were oozing with melted cheese and wilted courgette flowers cooked on the plancha. They use Swiss chard there when courgette flowers are out of season, or you could also use spinach.

SERVES FOUR TO SIX

2 tbsp olive oil
1 onion, finely sliced
1 finely chopped green jalapeño chilli or a good pinch of dried chilli flakes
1 clove garlic, finely chopped
250g courgette flowers, Swiss chard or spinach, washed and shredded
200g mozzarella, coarsely grated or thinly sliced
150g Lancashire cheese, crumbled
12 x 15cm *Blue corn tortillas* (page 44)
Salt, to taste

To serve
Roasted red tomato and chilli salsa (page 108) and/or
Stewed salsa verde (page 295)

Heat the oil in a saucepan and cook the onion, chopped chilli and garlic until soft but not coloured. Add the courgette flowers, chard or spinach to the pan with just the water that clings after washing. Allow the greens to wilt over the heat for a few minutes, while you grate or slice the cheese, then season with a little salt and the chilli flakes, if that's what you're using.

Lay a tortilla in a dry pan and sprinkle some of the mozzarella and Lancashire cheeses all over the surface. Add some of the courgette flower or greens mixture, then fold the tortilla in half to make a semi-circular parcel. Once the cheese is starting to melt, flip the quesadilla over and continue to cook until the cheese is oozing.

Remove the quesadilla from the pan and keep it warm while you make the rest. Cut into wedges and serve immediately with the salsas.

MEXICAN-STYLE CORN ON THE COB WITH CHILLI & MAYO

I ate a couple of elotes – one was simply not enough – in the Plaza de la Independencia, the central square of Mérida, one Sunday evening recently after we'd been filming jarana dancing in the late afternoon sun. Jarana is a mixture of Mayan and Spanish styles and the dancers are dressed immaculately, the men in white cotton suits with white hats, and the women in white dresses embellished with the famous Yucatán flower embroidery. We'd arrived that day and this dancing, which happens every Sunday, instantly put me in an 'I love Mérida' frame of mind, which hasn't diminished yet.
Try these on your barbecue.

SERVES FOUR

4 corn cobs, outer husks
  and silks removed
Oil, for brushing
1 lime, plus extra wedges
3–4 tbsp mayonnaise
50g Lancashire or feta
  cheese, crumbled
½ tsp chilli powder
  or Tabasco sauce
Salt, to taste

Heat your barbecue and brush the corn cobs with a little oil. Grill them over white-hot coals for 7–8 minutes, turning frequently with tongs until they're tender and with a few brown, charred spots.

Squeeze lime juice over the cooked cobs, then smother them in mayonnaise and crumbled cheese. Finish with a sprinkle of chilli powder or Tabasco and season with salt if needed. Eat straight away with extra lime wedges.

QUESADILLAS WITH SWEET POTATOES, CHORIZO & SWEETCORN

You can make quesadillas with flour or corn tortillas. Flour ones are easier to handle but the corn ones taste better. I've used flour tortillas here because there is quite a lot of filling which is harder to contain in corn ones. The mixture of sweet potato, chorizo and sweetcorn is not from a specific fast-food joint. It's just what Portia, Arezoo and I have brought together, having tried many a quesadilla all over Mexico.

Recipe photograph overleaf

SERVES FOUR

Corn oil
300g sweet potato, peeled
    and cut into 1.5cm dice
150g chorizo, skinned
    and finely chopped
150g fresh or frozen
    sweetcorn
4 spring onions, trimmed
    and sliced on an angle
1 jalapeño chilli, finely sliced
½ tsp dried oregano
½ tsp salt
6 turns black peppermill
4 large *Flour tortillas*
    (page 43 or bought)
300g mozzarella
    cheese, grated
Pico de gallo salsa
    (page 298)

Put your oven on at its lowest temperature. Heat a tablespoon of corn oil in a frying pan and fry the sweet potato and chorizo gently for about 10 minutes until they're browning at the edges. Add the sweetcorn, spring onions, chilli and oregano and cook for another few minutes, then season with salt and pepper.

Brush a large frying pan with a drizzle of oil, place it over a medium heat and lay a tortilla in the pan. Arrange a quarter of the sweet potato mixture over half the tortilla and top with a handful of the grated mozzarella. Fold the other half of the tortilla over the filling to make a semi-circle and cook for a few minutes until the cheese is starting to melt. Carefully turn the quesadilla over, using a fish slice or palette knife, and fry it on the other side for 3–4 minutes until it's golden and the cheese is oozing. Transfer it to the oven to keep warm while you make the rest. Serve cut into wedges with the salsa and a green salad.

'DROWNED' SANDWICHES WITH FRESH TOMATO SALSA & HOT RED CHILLI SAUCE

I was not attracted to the idea of a drowned soggy sandwich and it got worse when I went to the hole in the wall called Don José's place in Guadalajara, where they were being served up. They take a small sourdough baguette, known locally as a *birote*, slit it open and stuff it with fried carnitas. They then stick it in a plastic bag, ladle loads of fresh tomato sauce and chile de árbol sauce over it, sprinkle it with some sliced onion and give it to you. It's so sloppy that you have to sort of chew it out of the top of the bag. The fear is you might have ordered too much of the chilli sauce – you have to say quarter, half or full. Being that sort of person I ordered half and thanked my lucky stars I hadn't ordered more. It was blindingly hot. I duly sat down and started to slurp my sandwich out of the bag, then the transformation happened; it was completely delicious. I loved the combination of tart tomato sauce, hot chile de árbol sauce and lovely slow-roasted pork, but above all the way that the baguette, still warm from the bakery, had gone soft in some places, but remained crisp in others.

SERVES FOUR
400g *Carnitas* (page 86)
4 petit pain crusty rolls,
  sourdough if you can
  get them, warmed
Hot red chilli sauce
  (page 296) or Cholula sauce
1 small onion, finely sliced

For the fresh tomato salsa
12 ripe vine tomatoes
1 onion, roughly chopped
2 cloves garlic, chopped
1 red jalapeño chilli
1 tsp salt

Put all the ingredients for the fresh tomato salsa in a blender with 150ml of water and blend to a thin sauce.

Fry the carnitas in its own lard until browned and crisp around the edges. Slit the rolls down the middle and stuff them with carnitas. Sit the filled roll in a cereal bowl and ladle over a generous spoonful of tomato sauce, then 2–4 tablespoons of the hot sauce, according to taste. Add some sliced onion and eat immediately.

Alternatively, serve these in plastic bags, as they do on the streets of Mexico, with the sauces ladled on to the sandwiches and literally drowning them.

CHICKEN ENCHILADAS WITH SALSA VERDE

Cocina Económica Laurita is one of many cheap lunch places in the Azcapotzalco market, just north of the centre of Mexico City. The market is a bit like the one in Fez with very narrow passageways, and is slightly nerve wracking as it is so busy. At lunchtime it's crammed with locals queuing to get some of the best-value good food in the city. The queue was particularly long outside Laurita and I can understand why, as the dish I had there was superb and made so quickly by Saul. He was extremely amiable, especially considering the pressure he works under.

Most Mexicans would visit a place like this at least four times a week and they don't mess around. We were roundly ticked off by someone in the queue for daring to film them at lunch. Also, if you go, don't make the mistake of sitting at the tables of the next-door stalls. They don't like it! Once you've tasted the special green acidity of tomatillos it's hard to understand why they aren't part of our own cuisine, just like the tomato. *Recipe photograph overleaf*

SERVES FOUR

1 small chicken (1.35–1.5kg)
1 onion, roughly chopped
2 carrots, roughly chopped
2 cloves garlic, smashed
1 bay leaf
Sprig of thyme

For the salsa verde
1.5 kg tomatillos (or 1.4kg
   can of tomatillos, drained)
6 green serrano or
   jalapeño chillies,
   stems removed, halved
½ onion, chopped
2 cloves garlic, chopped
4 tbsp corn oil
1 tsp salt (you may need less
   if using tinned tomatillos)

To serve
12 x 15cm *Corn tortillas*
   (page 44 or bought)
100ml soured cream
60g Lancashire or feta
   cheese, crumbled
4 spring onions, finely sliced

Put the chicken in a pot with the onion, carrots, garlic, bay leaf and thyme and enough cold water to cover by about 5cm. Bring to the boil, then turn down the heat and poach the chicken gently for 30–40 minutes until cooked.

Remove the chicken and set it aside while you prepare the sauce. Continue to cook the stock with the vegetables for a further 15 minutes, then strain and boil rapidly until the liquid is reduced by half. Set it aside.

Put the tomatillos in a separate pan with about 600ml of water and the chillies. Bring to the boil and simmer for about 20 minutes until everything is tender and the tomatillos are pulpy. Add the onion and garlic, then about 250ml of the poaching liquid to loosen the consistency. Tip it all into a food processor and blend to a smooth sauce.

Heat the oil in the pan, add the sauce and season to taste. Simmer the sauce for 5 minutes or so more if it's too watery and you need to reduce it; add more stock if it's too thick.

Shred the chicken. Warm the tortillas (page 306), dip them into the sauce and arrange 3 on each plate. Fill the tortillas with the chicken, then fold them in half and douse them with more sauce. Top with soured cream, cheese and spring onions. Repeat to make the remaining servings.

CRAB TACOS WITH CHILLI, LIME & AVOCADO

I think these demonstrate the versatility of the corn tortilla. You can make larger ones with a really rich filling, like slow-cooked pork or lamb, or these small versions containing something delicate like fresh crab meat with tomato and avocado as a first course. Nothing is overpowering in this dish and I have mixed the crab with some mayonnaise to give it a little more richness. In my view, this is a perfect seafood starter and it's destined for The Seafood Restaurant in Padstow.

SERVES FOUR

12 x 10cm *Corn tortillas* (page 44 or bought)
250g white crab meat
3 tbsp mayonnaise
2 green serrano or jalapeño chillies (seeds in), cut in half and sliced
16 cherry tomatoes, quartered
1 little gem lettuce, finely shredded
2 limes, cut into wedges
2 avocados, stoned, peeled and sliced
Small handful coriander, chopped
Salt

Warm the tortillas in a dry frying pan, in a microwave or in the oven (page 306). Combine the crabmeat with the mayo. Pile the crab meat, chillies, tomatoes and lettuce on to the tortillas and top with lime wedges, slices of avocado and chopped coriander. Season with salt to taste.

EMPANADAS DE CAMARÓN
PRAWN EMPANADAS

One of the pleasures of Puerto Vallarta, which is on the Pacific coast of Mexico in the state of Jalisco, is joining the locals in their nightly 'paseo' along the wide boardwalk called El Malecón. The smell and the sound of the ocean as you stroll along in the early evening is very relaxing, and there's also the enticing thought that you can drop into many a restaurant, like Bar Oceano, and have a snack with your margarita or Pacifico beer. These prawn empanadas – little pastry turnovers stuffed with prawns and tomato – are the sort of dish you will get. What makes them very special is the pastry, which is made with a spicy red chilli sauce, such as Cholula.

MAKES ABOUT SIXTEEN EMPANADAS

For the dough
500g maize flour
½ tsp salt
95ml Huichol, Cholula or
  hot chilli sauce of choice
About 350ml water

For the filling
30g butter
1 tsp olive oil
1 onion, finely chopped
2 large carrots,
  finely chopped
2 tomatoes, finely chopped
250g raw prawns
  (peeled weight), chopped
Salt and pepper, to taste

To cook and serve
1–1.5 litres corn
  or vegetable oil
Shredded romaine
  or iceberg lettuce
Chilli sauce
Soured cream
Small handful coriander,
  roughly chopped

Sift the flour and salt into a bowl. Make a well in the centre and add the sauce and 200ml of the water. Mix, adding some or all of the remaining water until you have a soft, malleable but not sticky dough. Wrap the dough in cling film and chill.

For the filling, heat the butter and oil in a pan. Add the onion and carrots and sweat them for 5 minutes, then add the tomatoes and cook for a few minutes to reduce any excess liquid. Add the prawns and stir until they have turned opaque and pink. Season to taste. Allow the filling to cool completely before making the empanandas or the dough will be hard to work with – any heat makes the pastry crack and fall apart.

When everything is cold, divide the dough into 16 balls, then make them into discs like tortillas. Use a tortilla press if you have one, or put each piece of dough between two sheets of plastic and roll it out with a rolling pin.

Lay a disc of dough on a sheet of plastic. Add a tablespoon of filling on one half, then using the plastic, fold the dough over to form a half-moon shape. Press the edges to seal, then peel off the plastic and set the empanada aside while you make the rest.

Heat some oil in a large pan – the oil should be about 5cm deep. Lower one or two empanadas into the oil and fry them for about 3 minutes each side. Remove them with a slotted spoon and drain them on kitchen paper. Keep them warm while you fry the rest. Serve with lettuce, chilli sauce, soured cream and coriander.

TACOS DE PESCADO ESTILO ENSENADA
ENSENADA FISH TACOS WITH CHILLI & CORIANDER

For many years the beaches on the north coast of Cornwall were patrolled by Australian lifeguards, originally because they had the surf life-saving skills that were unfamiliar to the locals. For me, this meant many summers of friendship with pleasant Australians, all of whom seemed to be sunny and optimistic. Well, you would be, wouldn't you, with a summer in Cornwall and lots of locals finding you irresistible? One such lifeguard was Rudi, who used to return year after year. Everyone was extremely fond of him – so much so that we filmed a little sequence about a trip he'd made to Ensenada on the Baja California coast, where they made fabulous fish tacos. We cooked some on the beach in Cornwall by the lifeguard hut, and Rudi took Chalky, my Jack Russell, out for a little surfing lesson. Sadly, when back in Australia five years later, Rudi died of cancer and I always thought that one day I'd get to Ensenada and find the tacos.

SERVES SIX

12 x 15cm *Corn tortillas*
   (page 44 or bought)
600g cod fillet
100g plain flour, seasoned
   with pinch of salt and
   6 turns black peppermill
1 litre corn or vegetable oil

For the batter
200g plain flour
¼ tsp salt
½ tsp baking powder
275ml ice-cold beer

For the toppings
¼ small white cabbage,
   finely shredded
1 avocado, stoned,
   peeled and diced
Pico de gallo salsa (page 298)
Hot chilli sauce, such as
   Cholula or Huichol

For the chipotle crema
2 *Chipotles en adobo*
   (page 298 or bought)
3 tbsp mayonnaise
3 tbsp soured cream
Juice of ½ lime

Warm the tortillas in a dry frying pan, in a microwave or in the oven (page 306). Get your toppings – shredded cabbage, diced avocado, pico de gallo salsa, and hot chilli sauce – ready. Mix the ingredients for the crema and set aside.

To make the batter, sift the flour, salt and baking powder into a roomy bowl. Using a balloon whisk, incorporate the beer until you have a smooth batter. Set aside.

Cut the fish into fingers about 1cm thick. Heat the oil in a large pan to 190°C. Dip a few pieces of fish into the seasoned flour, shake off the excess, then dip them into the batter. Fry for 2–2½ minutes until crisp and golden. Repeat until you've cooked all the fish, draining each batch briefly on kitchen paper to remove excess oil. Sprinkle lightly with salt.

Serve the fish immediately in warm tortillas, with the toppings on the table for guests to help themselves.

ANTOJITOS Y GARNACHAS
ENSENADA
70

BATTERED MACKEREL WITH MAYO, CHILLI SAUCE & LIME

In the Nueva Viga fish market in Mexico City, the second-largest fish market in the world after Tsukiji in Tokyo, the most popular street food enjoyed by stallholders and shoppers alike is fillets of sierra, a type of mackerel. The fillets are deep-fried in beer batter, split open and slathered in mayonnaise, lime, salt and chilli sauce. It's right up there with the grilled mackerel in a baguette with chilli and sumac they serve on the Bosphorus in Istanbul.

SERVES FOUR

4 very fresh mackerel
   fillets, all bones removed
1 litre corn oil

For the batter
200g plain flour
½ tsp salt
1½ tsp baking powder
275ml ice-cold beer

To serve
Fine salt
2 limes, cut into wedges
150ml mayonnaise,
   preferably Kewpie
   in a squeezy bottle
Hot chilli sauce, such as
   Cholula or Salsa Huichol
   or even Tabasco

Sift the flour, salt and baking powder into a roomy bowl, then whisk in the ice-cold beer to make a thick and smooth batter. Put your oven on at a low setting, about 120°C.

Add the oil to a pan wide enough to accommodate the mackerel fillets and heat to 185°C. Dip a mackerel fillet into the batter, lower it into the hot oil and fry for 4–5 minutes until golden and crisp. Drain the fillet on kitchen paper and keep it warm in the oven while cooking the rest.

When all the fillets are ready, slit them along their length. Sprinkle them with salt, squeeze the lime wedges over them and then squirt with mayonnaise and chilli sauce.

PRAWN AGUACHILE TOSTADAS WITH WATERMELON ESCABECHE

The Criollo Taquería in Ensenada is the one place in town you need to head for if you want to taste a new and lively interpretation of Mexican cuisine. Memo Baretto and Tania Livier, the young couple who own and run it, are definitely going places. In fact I think I was lucky to eat there when I did because I suspect in a few years they'll be quite famous and somewhere bigger. As it is, this place is pretty trendy – mostly outdoors, a lot of black and stainless steel, very smart denim aprons, black T-shirts – with food to match. I particularly liked this dish of raw prawns (cooked in lime juice), with watermelon escabeche, chilli, onion and tomato and a liberal application of the avocado sauce, guacatillo, which is made with ripe avocados, tomatillos, green chilli and coriander. I really like Ensenada, but going to the Criollo Taquería you wonder whether the town is quite ready for such youthful talent.

SERVES FOUR

For the escabeche
watermelon
  (400g prepared weight)
125ml white wine vinegar
25g granulated sugar
1 tsp salt
2 chiles de árbol
3 allspice berries
2 slices lemon

For the prawns
300g raw prawns,
  peeled and deveined
30ml fresh lime juice
½ jalapeño, sliced into rounds
1 small red onion, finely sliced
8 cherry tomatoes, quartered
16 thin slices cucumber
½ tsp salt
2 tbsp olive oil

To serve
300ml corn oil
4 *Corn tortillas* (page 44)
Guacatillo sauce (page 296)
3–4 radishes, finely sliced
Small handful coriander,
  roughly chopped
1 tbsp olive oil

For the escabeche, cut the watermelon into wedges and remove the skin and seeds. Cut the wedges into smaller pieces, then set aside. Mix the vinegar with the sugar, salt, chiles de árbol, allspice berries and 100ml of water. Add the watermelon and lemon slices, then set aside for an hour. You'll have more escabeche than you need, but you can use it another time.

Put the prawns in a bowl and pour over the lime juice, then chill them in the fridge for 20–30 minutes. Add the sliced jalapeño, red onion, tomatoes, cucumber slices and salt. Drizzle with the olive oil, then stir in the pickled watermelon. Discard the lemon slices.

Heat the oil to 180°C in a frying pan and fry the tortillas for a minute. Drain them on kitchen paper. On each tortilla, put one-quarter of the prawn mixture, drizzle with guacatillo sauce, then garnish with sliced radishes and coriander. Finish with a few drops of olive oil, then serve.

CHICKEN BURRITOS WITH PICO DE GALLO SALSA

When I test recipes for my cookery books I like to work with Portia Spooner in the cottage in Padstow, and I ring up The Seafood Restaurant and ask for a particularly bright young chef to come and give us a hand. This time head chef Stephane Delourme was deeply apologetic but couldn't spare anyone. My son Jack, who's now following in his dad's footsteps and making TV cookery shows called 'Born to Cook', suggested his girlfriend Lucy Musca. He said, 'She's done a bit of cooking', so I thought better somebody than nobody. She's Aussie but turns out to be half-Italian and does anyone know anyone who's half-Italian who can't cook, because I certainly don't! And more to the point she casually mentioned that she used to have a Mexican streetfood taco stand in Oxford, of all places. This recipe is fab and much as I bang on about the wonderfulness of corn tortillas, flour ones do have their place. They are much better for bigger fillings like this one, and the gluten content in the flour makes for a proper wrap.

MAKES FOUR

4 chicken thighs, boned
4 large *Flour tortillas*
   (page 43 or bought)
200–250g cooked rice
Guacamole (page 105)
Pico de gallo salsa (page 298)
Handful grated mozzarella
4 tbsp soured cream
½ little gem lettuce,
   shredded
Chipotle crema (page 298)

For the marinade
Juice of 2 limes
2 cloves garlic, crushed
60ml olive oil
1 heaped tsp oregano
1 tsp chilli flakes
1 tsp brown sugar
Salt and pepper

Mix the marinade ingredients in a bowl, add the chicken thighs, then cover and leave them for 2 hours or longer in the fridge.

Seal the chicken thighs in a hot pan for a few minutes. When they are browned, add the marinade to the pan, cover and leave the chicken to cook through for 10–15 minutes. Slice the chicken into strips.

Lay the tortillas on a board and layer up the fillings – rice, guacamole, mozzarella, soured cream, lettuce and chipotle crema. Fold up the bottom of each tortilla, then fold the sides in and roll the tortilla up to contain the filling. Cut it in half to serve.

TAMALES DE TINGA
CHICKEN TINGA TAMALES

When I first went to Mexico in 1968 I found tamales boring and it wasn't until a trip to Puerta Vallarta about three years ago that I realised there is a point to them – and the point is always the filling. I tracked this recipe down to a family business, way out of the tourist area in PV, and discovered that the secret of Maria Elena's tamales was chicken tinga – slow-cooked chicken with tomato and chipotle. Maria Elena explained that the crucial thing was the lightness of her tamal dough. Maybe, but the corn dough flavoured with lard and chicken stock is like the most wonderful suet dumpling and combines with the delicious smoky flavour of the chicken to make a memorable dish. Extraordinarily, I am now quite happy to eat less perfect combinations like rajas (poblano and onion) or prawn, borracho pork and jalapeño chillies.

MAKES 24 TO 28 TAMALES (SERVES EIGHT TO TEN)

24–28 corn husks
½ quantity of *Chicken tinga* (page 204), cold
Stewed salsa verde (page 295) or salsa of choice

For the dough
500g tamal masa flour (coarser than regular maize tortilla flour)
1½–2 tsp salt (depending on saltiness of stock)
2 tsp baking powder
220g lard, melted
700–750ml *Chicken stock* (page 300) or poaching liquor from the chicken tinga

Soak the husks in a bowl of just-boiled water. Weigh them down to keep them submerged and leave for an hour or two.

To make the dough, put the flour, salt and baking powder in a food mixer. With the food mixer on a medium speed, add the melted lard and mix until incorporated. With the mixer still running, add three quarters of the stock, then the rest a little at a time. Beat for 4–5 minutes until the dough has the consistency of cake batter – soft but holding its shape. You can refrigerate it at this stage for an hour or two, then beat again prior to using.

Drain the corn husks and dry them with a tea towel. With the narrow end of a husk nearest you, spread 2–3 tablespoons of dough in the centre of the husk with the back of a spoon. It should make a 10–12cm square and be about ½cm thick. Leaving a border around the edge, spoon about 1½ tablespoons of cold chicken tinga in the centre of the dough. Using the corn husk, wrap the dough over the filling to encase it. Fold the sides over each other and the narrower end up, then tie with string to form an open-topped parcel. Repeat to make the rest.

Boil some water in a large steamer or a fish kettle. Arrange the wrapped tamales upright, with open end uppermost, in the steaming basket and steam them for 45–50 minutes or until the dough comes away from the husk easily. Make sure you keep the water level topped up. Allow the tamales to sit for 5–8 minutes or so to firm up a little before serving. Serve 3 per person with a salsa of your choice.

CHAR-GRILLED BEEF TACOS WITH SPRING ONIONS & GUACAMOLE

There is an avenue right in the middle of the Mercado de 20 Novembre in Oaxaca, that is wreathed in smoke right up to the vaulted corrugated iron roofs. There must be twenty charcoal grills creating an inferno of smoke. Each stall displays sheets of thin, lightly salted beef and they sell little pork sausages and escalopes of pork too, orange-hued and rubbed with powdered chilli. At other stalls you buy the corn tortillas, guacamole, spring onions, coriander and tomato salsa. You get the onions grilled along with the beef or pork, and then you sit at long white, Formica-topped tables with a pile of tortillas to make ever-varying combinations of the chewy but well-flavoured beef that tastes of the fire, the guacamole, onion and chilli. You rub shoulders with cheerful, reassuringly well-fed Mexicans and drink Corona or Victoria beer. This recipe is based on that whole experience. I wrote this piece for my book *Coast to Coast* some years ago and I was lucky enough to have the same dish in Oaxaca earlier this year. Everything I said was still the same, right down to the beers.

SERVES EIGHT

900g rump of beef, very
    thinly sliced by your
    butcher into about
    12 slices
Salt
15 large salad onions,
    trimmed and halved
    lengthways or 30
    whole spring onions
Olive or corn oil, for brushing
16–24 x 15cm *Corn tortillas*
    (page 44 or bought)
Guacamole (page 105)
Roasted red tomato and
    chilli salsa (page 108)

Lightly sprinkle each slice of beef with ¼ teaspoon of salt and set them aside for about 10 minutes. Heat a griddle pan over a high heat until it's smoking hot. Brush the onions and beef lightly with oil.

Griddle the onions for 2–3 minutes, then transfer them to a serving plate and keep them warm. Griddle a few of the beef slices for about 20 seconds per side, then slice them into strips. Warm the tortillas in a dry frying pan, in a microwave or in the oven (page 306). Serve with the beef, guacamole, salsa and lime wedges. Continue to cook the remaining slices of beef while your guests start eating.

CARNITAS
SLOW-COOKED PORK TACOS WITH CORIANDER & SALSA ROJA

Even though we weren't in Mexico, we found that these carnitas from the Taquería Vallarta in the Mission District, San Francisco, were extremely good. There was no chance of the very busy Mexican cooks giving me the recipe, but it was more the accompaniments that made them so special. I had ducked into the restaurant from a somewhat chaotic Mexican festival celebrating the life of Cesar Chevez, the campaigner for migrant workers. This included a procession of immaculately restored American cars from the 60s and 70s, with lowered suspension and fat tyres carefully engineered to raise the front or back hydraulically. I was told later this was a passion around Mexicali, the capital of Baja California. To an outsider it was bizarre, but the audience was massively enthusiastic. Carnitas is pork simmered very slowly in lard until it is meltingly tender. It's very similar to French confit. This is my interpretation of a number of similar versions from the state of Michoacán. The recipes often include orange juice to cut the richness.

SERVES FOUR TO SIX

1kg boned pork shoulder, cut into 6cm chunks
½ medium onion, chopped
2 cloves garlic, chopped
2 tsp dried oregano
1½ tsp salt
250g lard
125ml whole milk
125ml fresh orange juice

For the tortillas and garnishes
20 x 15cm *Corn tortillas* (page 44 or bought)
Handful coriander, roughly chopped
Handful radishes, sliced
½ medium onion, chopped
2 limes, cut into wedges
Stewed salsa verde (page 295)
Roasted red tomato and chilli salsa (page 108)

Put the diced pork in a casserole dish with the onion, garlic, oregano, salt, lard, milk and orange juice. Cover the dish and simmer for about 45 minutes, then remove the lid and cook for a further 1¼ hours until the meat is meltingly tender.

Remove the pork with a slotted spoon, and pull the meat apart with two forks. Continue to simmer the juices until the liquid has all but evaporated. The fat will have separated and will be sitting on the top so you can ladle it out to use again for cooking more carnitas, refried beans or delicious fried potatoes.

Scrape all the solids from the bottom of the pan and pour the reduced juices and solids over the shredded pork. Stir to combine. Use the meat as a filling for tacos, burritos, tostadas, ahogados, sliders and tamales.

TACOS WITH KIMCHI

Another way of eating carnitas is in tortillas, topped with Korean kimchi and a teaspoon of Gochujang (Korean red chilli paste), now available in large supermarkets.

TACOS AL PASTOR

DONER TACOS WITH PINEAPPLE & SALSA

Tacos al pastor originated in the Lebanon. The Lebanese brought the doner kebab, a large cone-shaped joint of pressed meat cooked on a vertical rotisserie, to Mexico but what was lamb became pork. The best ones I've had there were at a place called El Vilsito, which was a garage by day and then transformed into a taquería in the evening. It was a joy to watch the cooks slicing the pork on to tortillas, then deftly reaching up and scything off a morsel from a pineapple stuck on the very top of the barbecue. So skilled were they that they were able to cut a slice of pineapple and have it drop straight into the taco in one movement. Obviously at home you can't create a mini donor, so I suggest marinating thinly sliced pork loin and cooking it quickly under the grill.

SERVES FOUR TO SIX

4 dried guajillo chillies, cleaned and seeds shaken out, cut into 3 or 4
60ml pineapple juice, from a tin, bottle or carton
3 cloves garlic, peeled
60ml cider vinegar
25g achiote paste
½ onion, chopped
1 tsp dried oregano
¼ tsp ground cumin
1 tsp salt
900g pork shoulder steaks, about 1.5cm thick, with some fat
1 small fresh pineapple or 425g tin of pineapple slices in juice

To serve
12–16 x 15cm *Corn tortillas* (page 44 or bought)
1 quantity *Roasted red tomato and chilli salsa* (page 108)
1 small onion, chopped
Handful of coriander, chopped

Put the dried chillies in a bowl and cover them with about 250ml of just-boiled water. Cover the bowl with cling film and let the chillies soften for about 20 minutes.

Put the chillies in a food processor with 5–6 tablespoons of their soaking liquor. Add the pineapple juice, garlic, vinegar, achiote paste, onion, oregano and cumin, then blend until you have a smooth marinade. Season with salt. Put the pork steaks in a bowl, pour the marinade over them and massage it into the meat. Cover the bowl with cling film and put it in the fridge for 3–4 hours.

Preheat your grill to medium and cook the steaks for about 7 minutes on each side. If using a barbecue, it's best to cook the steaks in foil to avoid burning the marinade.

Once the meat is cooked through, leave it to rest for 10 minutes, covered with foil. If using fresh pineapple, peel and core it and cut it into slices 1cm thick. If using tinned, drain the slices. Increase the heat to medium/high and cook the pineapple slices on both sides until browned and charred around the edges.

Warm the tortillas in a dry frying pan, in a microwave or the oven (page 306). Cut the pork into thin strips and the pineapple into chunks, and serve both in tortillas. Top with salsa, chopped onion and coriander.

COCHINITA PIBIL
SLOW-COOKED PORK WITH ACHIOTE & ORANGE

This Yucatán dish of slow-cooked pork with brick-red achiote paste and sour orange juice is eaten throughout Mexico in tacos. Traditionally, the Mayans wrapped the meat in banana leaves and cooked it in a pit in the ground. These days it is often cooked in the oven, but aficionados say that they can tell the difference. The sour orange juice is an important element in the dish so use Seville oranges if possible. Problem is they are seasonal but you can do a pibil at other times of year with regular oranges. Pibil is normally served as a taco filling with pink pickled onions and lime juice, plus roasted red tomato and chilli salsa. In true Yucatán style you can add some habaneros in place of jalapeños to your salsa for extra heat.

SERVES SIX

1.5kg boned pork shoulder,
  cut into 3–4 pieces
Salt
3 cloves garlic, unpeeled
5cm cinnamon stick
1 tsp black peppercorns
4 allspice berries
2 whole cloves
1 tsp cumin seeds
60g achiote paste
1½ tsp fine salt
1 tsp hot chilli powder
1 tsp dried oregano
1 tsp thyme leaves
250ml Seville orange juice
  or ordinary orange juice
1 small onion, thinly sliced

To serve
30 x 15cm *Corn tortillas*
  (page 44 or bought)
Lime wedges
Pink pickled onions
  (page 296)
*Roasted red tomato and
  chilli salsa* (page 108)

Rub the pork all over with the salt and set aside. To make the marinade, heat a dry, heavy-based frying pan and roast the garlic cloves. Once they are browned, set them aside, then toast the cinnamon stick, peppercorns, allspice berries, cloves and cumin seeds. In a pestle and mortar or spice grinder grind all the marinade ingredients. Add the achiote paste, 1½ teaspoons of fine salt, chilli powder, oregano and thyme leaves and mix well with the orange juice. Roll the pork in the marinade, rubbing it in well. Cover the bowl with cling film and leave it in the fridge for 4–6 hours or overnight.

Preheat the oven to 160°C/Fan 140°C. Place the pork in a casserole dish with all the marinade on top. Arrange the sliced onion on the meat, and put a lid on the casserole. Bake for 3½–4 hours, checking it a couple of times during cooking and adding a little water if the meat looks as though it is drying out.

When cooked the meat should be very tender and moist. Pull it apart with a couple of forks and mix it with the marinade and juices in the casserole dish. Serve with warm tortillas, lime wedges, pink pickled onions and salsa.

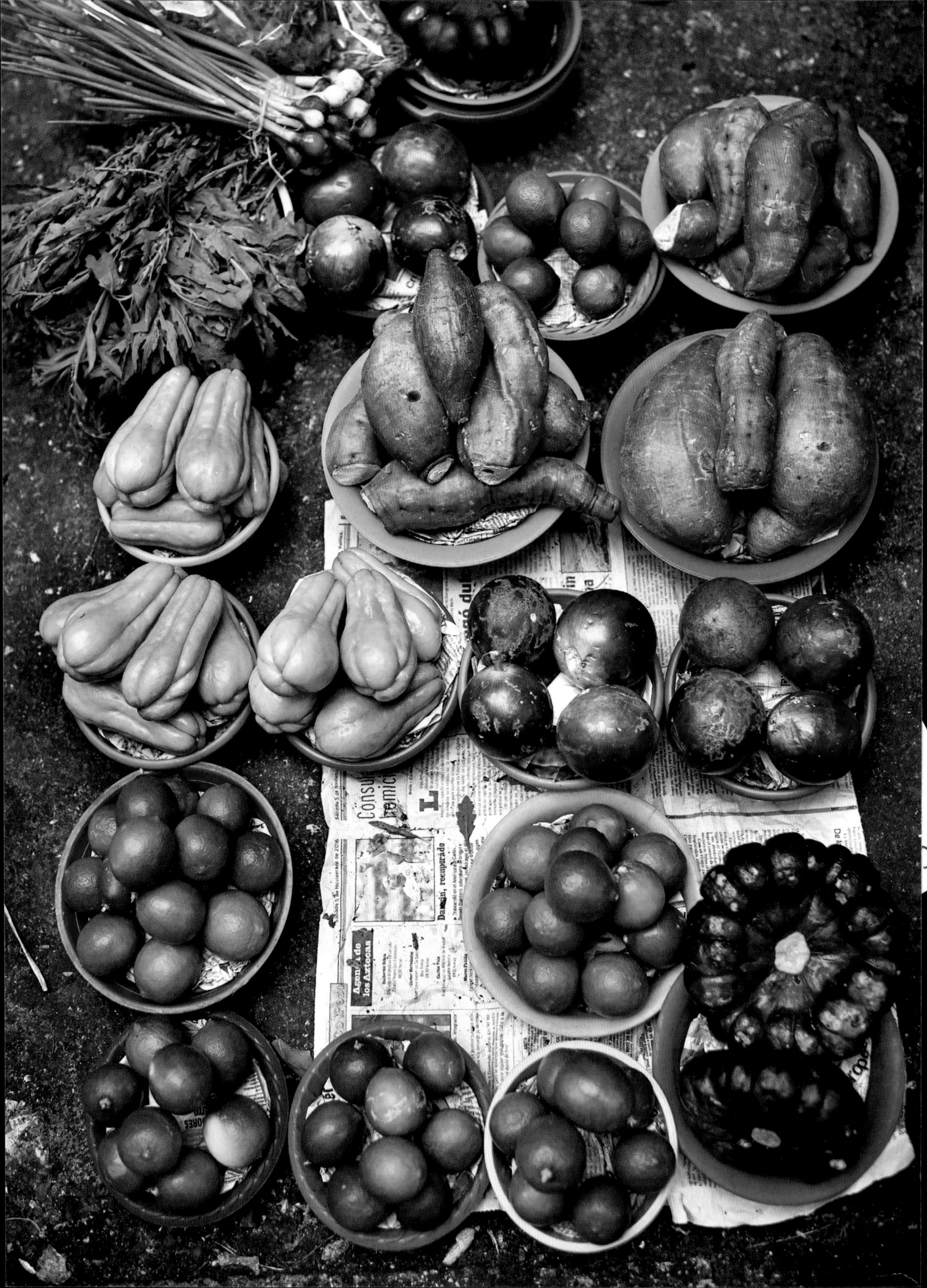
Damián, recuperado
Agenda de los Aztecas

ENSALADAS, VERDURAS y GUARNICIONES

VEGETABLES & SIDES

If you're ever in Oaxaca on a Sunday and you can tear yourself away from one of Mexico's most attractive cities, there's good reason to visit the Tianguis market in the town of Tlacolula about 45 minutes away. This little market, where farmers come from all around to sell their produce, is a journey into the heart of Mexican country life. It was this part of Mexico where corn is believed to have been first cultivated many thousands of years ago, so it's natural that corn should be so evident in the market, not just golden in hue but blue, white, green and almost black. There's a warm corn drink called atole on sale, and many food stalls selling blue corn quesadillas stuffed with cheese, onions and courgette flowers. The shades of corn are mesmerising, but the arrays of fresh and dried chillies are also amazing for their variety and colours, not just the red, green, orange and lemon-yellow fresh ones but the dried varieties, ranging from dull red through brown to the deepest black anchos and mulatos. The warm fruity scent of dried chillies in the morning sun is reason enough to be there.

There's a feeling of being in a much older Mexico. Most of the produce is pre-Hispanic in origin – corn, chillies, tomatoes, tomatillos, chocolate, even the livestock. The people are almost pure Zapotec – not much Spanish influence there. It serves to remind one that Mexican cooking, like Chinese or Indian, has ancient roots (Mesoamerican it's called) and the conquest by the Spanish in the 16th century when cattle, sheep, pigs and goats as well as flour and dairy produce were introduced, enriched an already sophisticated cuisine.

There's a vegan restaurant in Hollywood called Gracias Madre; I have a recipe for cauliflower fritters (page 136) from there. It's extremely successful and the food is very good, all based on the idea of the importance to the whole of the Americas of the produce from such markets and the importance of the women of Mexico in traditional cooking. The meaning of Gracias Madre is 'thanks to our mother'.

BLACK BEANS WITH GARLIC, ONION & BAY LEAF

Black beans are used throughout Mexico for refried beans, but also in soups, stews and salsas. Most black beans don't need pre-soaking but check the packet just in case.

SERVES FOUR

300g black turtle beans
  or pinto beans
1 onion, peeled and halved
4 cloves garlic, bashed
  with the heel of a knife
1 bay leaf
1 tsp salt

Rinse the beans very well and pick out any stones. Tip them into a large saucepan and cover with about 2 litres of water, then add the onion, garlic, bay leaf and salt, then bring to the boil. Skim off any scum that rises to the top and continue to boil, uncovered, for 10 minutes.

Turn the heat down and simmer the beans gently for up to an hour or until the beans are tender but not disintegrating.

Drain and reserve about 150ml of the cooking liquid to use if you going to make refried beans (page 104).

GUACAMOLE

There's no such thing as a standard recipe for guacamole. I asked the chef Alejandro Ruiz to make the definitive one at his farm just outside Oaxaca and was surprised when he put only avocado, onion, coriander and salt into the mortar and pestle. I was thinking that surely he'd add some lime juice, but he said this was the way everyone makes it there. I've seen guacamole made with tomatoes, sometimes chillies, sometimes with coriander and sometimes not. The only vital ingredient seems to be the avocado itself. Guacamole means a mole made from avocado. The word avocado comes from the Nahuatl *ahuacatl*, which was also often used by the Aztecs to describe testicles – and when you consider the shape you can see what they meant. This recipe was given to me by Diana Kennedy, the revered English cookery writer on all things Mexican, when I visited her in Michoacán about 17 years ago. It's a really good one and I always remember her saying, 'You must leave the mixture a bit lumpy.'

SERVES FOUR
1 jalapeño or serrano
   green chilli, deseeded
   and finely chopped
½ small white onion,
   finely chopped
¼ tsp salt
1 large ripe avocado
   or 2 small, stoned
   and peeled
Juice of ½–1 lime
1 small handful
   coriander, chopped
Totopos (page 299),
   to serve

Pound the chopped chilli in a pestle and mortar with the onion and salt. When they're broken down to a lumpy paste, add the avocado and break up the flesh roughly with a fork.

Stir in the lime juice to taste and the chopped coriander. Serve immediately with totopos.

ROASTED RED TOMATO & CHILLI SALSA

This is a great all-round salsa for serving at the table as a topping for a multitude of tacos, totopos and so on. What differentiates this tomato and chilli salsa from any other chilli sauce is the fact that the vegetables are charred before being pounded. This gives a subtle toasted flavour to an otherwise uncooked salsa. Roasting chillies, normally over charcoal, is a very common preparation for many a Mexican dish.

SERVES EIGHT TO TEN

4 ripe plum tomatoes
2 cloves garlic, skin on
1 whole red jalapeño
   or serrano chilli
¼ tsp salt
1 small onion, finely chopped
Juice of ½–1 lime (to taste)
Small handful of coriander,
   freshly chopped

Heat a dry heavy-based frying pan until hot. Add the tomatoes, garlic and chilli and roast them until they're softened and have brown patches all over them. Remove the garlic and chilli first. You can roast all the ingredients in a 200°C/Fan 180°C oven for 15–20 minutes, but the frying pan method is more authentic.

Roughly chop the tomatoes when they're cool enough to handle. Peel the garlic and put it in a pestle and mortar with the chilli (stem removed). Bash to break them up, then add the tomatoes and salt and continue bashing until you have a thick pulpy sauce. Alternatively, you can pulse everything in a blender to this point. Stir in the chopped onion, lime juice to taste and the chopped coriander.

Serve with dishes such as tacos, eggs and totopos.

PATTI'S GREEN BEANS

On a trip to the Chinantla Region of Oaxaca I spent a day tracking down wild vanilla with the gatherers, who are so expert they can smell the pods in the forest. The plant is a type of orchid and the vine extends for 50 metres or more. The orchid gatherers farm coffee in the same area, and after a morning in the jungle gathering vanilla and coffee we repaired to the little village of Rancho Grande. Our hosts Patti and Hector gave us lunch, which included this simple side dish of green beans with tomatoes, garlic and jalapeño chilli.

**SERVES FOUR
AS A SIDE DISH**

400g green beans, trimmed
2 large ripe tomatoes, quartered
1 garlic clove
1 small onion, quartered
1 red jalapeño chilli, stem removed (seeds in or out)
2 tbsp olive oil
½ tsp salt
½ tsp caster sugar (optional)

Bring a pan of water to the boil, add the green beans and blanch them for a minute, then drain. Cut them into 2cm lengths and set aside.

Put the tomatoes, garlic, onion and jalapeño in a blender and liquidise them. Heat the olive oil in a saucepan, then add the contents of the blender – watch out, as the mixture may spit and splatter at first. Heat and stir for 2 minutes, then add the green beans and salt.

Taste and if the tomatoes are not very ripe and sweet you may want to add a little sugar. Stir and continue to simmer for about 10–15 minutes until the beans are tender. If the sauce starts to dry out, add a splash of water. Taste for seasoning and add a little more salt if you want.

TORTILLA SOUP WITH CHIPOTLE CHILLI, TOMATO & AVOCADO

As a restaurateur, I know how hard it is to persuade people to go for the soup. This is because often you get a bowl of just that. If you want people to order soup, you have to make it special by adding lots of garnishes or bringing to the table in a tureen or jug and ladling it out. In Mexico, as with so many other dishes, soup is all about the bits that you add – in this case, avocado, chilli flakes, coriander and often a lick of soured cream. It's usual to make this with pasilla chillies, but I had some made with chipotle in a back street near Cholula Market and very nice it was too. I've also had sopa Azteca with extra shredded meat from a cooked chicken and even crisp pieces of chicken or pork skin. I often just order the soup off the menu and find it a perfect light supper all on its own. *Recipe photograph overleaf*

SERVES FOUR

8 large ripe tomatoes
2 cloves garlic
2–3 tbsp lard
2 onions, sliced
2 tbsp *Chipotles en adobo*
  (page 298 or bought)
1 tsp dried oregano
1 litre home-made chicken
  or vegetable stock
1½ tsp salt
8 turns black peppermill
220g cooked chicken,
  shredded (optional)
4 x 15cm *Corn tortillas*
  (page 44 or bought),
  cut into 1cm strips
500ml corn or vegetable oil

For the garnishes
1½ tsp dried chipotle flakes
1 avocado, stoned, peeled,
  diced and tossed in
  lime juice
75g Lancashire or feta
  cheese, crumbled
100g soured cream
Small handful of freshly
  chopped coriander

Heat a dry, heavy-based pan and roast the tomatoes and garlic until charred. Set them aside to cool, then peel both.

Heat the lard in a saucepan and gently cook the onions until softened but not coloured. Add the peeled garlic and cook for a further 4–5 minutes. Add the chipotles, peeled tomatoes and oregano, then the stock and cook for 10–15 minutes until everything is soft and pulpy. Liquidise until smooth. Season with salt and pepper, add the shredded chicken, if using, and keep the soup warm over a low heat.

Pour the oil into a frying pan to a depth of about 2.5cm. Heat the oil and fry the tortilla strips in batches until golden and crisp. Remove the strips with a slotted spoon and drain them on kitchen paper.

Serve the soup with strips of tortilla on top and a sprinkling of chipotle flakes, diced avocado, cheese, soured cream and coriander.

RAJAS CON CREMA
FRIED POBLANO CHILLIES WITH ONIONS & CREAM

Served as a filling for tacos or tamales or as a vegetable side, this dish is simple but really delicious. Traditionally it's made with poblano chillies but you can substitute green peppers, with a little green jalapeño or serrano chilli for a touch of heat. You can also add some sweetcorn, which leaves you with a delicious dilemma – is less more or is the sweetcorn something that should always be part of a rajas?

SERVES THREE TO FOUR

5 poblano chillies
   or 4 green peppers
   and 1 green jalapeño
   or serrano chilli,
   finely sliced
30g butter
1 medium onion,
   finely sliced
150ml soured cream
1 tsp salt

Getting some charred flavour of grilled chillies or green peppers is an important element of this dish. This is best done on the barbecue or you can char the chillies or peppers under your grill. Give them an initial burn over a gas flame if you have one, or use a blowtorch, then put them under the grill (or broiler as the Americans call it). Whether you're using a barbecue or grill, cook the chillies or peppers for about 12 minutes, turning them frequently. Leave them to cool, then remove the skin, stem and seeds and cut the flesh into 5mm strips.

Melt the butter in a frying pan over a low to medium heat. Add the onion, and fry it until golden, then add the poblano or green pepper strips, stir well and cook for 2 minutes. Add the soured cream and salt to the pan and cook for another minute or two.

The dish is now ready to eat as an accompaniment to tacos, quesadillas and so on. If using this as a filling for tamales, let it cool, then stir in grated mozzarella or a couple of handfuls of sweetcorn before filling the corn husks.

STUFFED ANCHO CHILLIES WITH GOAT'S CHEESE & TOMATO SAUCE

I loved the restaurant El Mural in the centre of Puebla. The name refers to the large mural on the wall which features a sort of Sergeant Pepper group of local dignitaries, journalists, poets, historical figures and revolutionaries, all appearing to be having a wonderful time in some gigantic imaginary banquet. The chef is called Liz Galicia and with a name like Liz and a surname that seemed to come from northern Spain, I was quite surprised to learn that her family seem to have come from Puebla forever. I thoroughly enjoyed this stuffed chilli dish, which was perfectly executed, subtle and not overpowering in any way. Ancho chillies, which are the dried version of the extremely mild, large green poblano chillies, are quite easy to get hold of in the UK. *Recipe photograph overleaf*

SERVES SIX

For the stuffed chillies
300g soft goat's cheese
250g ricotta or curd cheese
½ tsp salt
12 turns black peppermill
2 tbsp olive oil
½ onion, chopped
4 cloves garlic, bashed
6 ancho chillies
   (dried poblano chillies)
2 bay leaves
1 tsp dried oregano
2 tsp soft brown sugar
Coriander sprigs, for garnish

For the tomato sauce
3 dried guajillo chillies,
   stems removed and
   seeds shaken out
6 large plum tomatoes,
   roughly chopped
1 tsp tomato purée
½ large onion, quartered
6 cloves garlic, bashed
½ tsp dried epazote
   (optional) or oregano
2 tbsp olive oil
Salt

First make the tomato sauce. Soak the guajillo chillies for 20 minutes in just-boiled water, then drain them.

Place the tomatoes, tomato purée, soaked chillies, onion, garlic and epazote or oregano in a pan with 350ml of water. Cook for about 15–20 minutes, then pour into a blender and blend until smooth. Heat the oil in a pan and sieve in the liquidised sauce. Season with salt and cook gently over a low heat for about 10 minutes. Set it aside until ready to serve.

Mash the cheeses in a bowl and season with salt and black pepper.

Heat the olive oil in pan and fry the onion, garlic and chillies. After a few minutes, add the bay leaves, oregano, sugar and enough water to cover (about 600ml). Simmer the chillies gently for 15–20 minutes until tender, then remove them to a colander and leave to cool. Discard the onion, garlic and herbs. Preheat the oven to 180°C/Fan 160°C.

When the chillies are cool enough to handle, score down the length of one with a small sharp knife, making sure you do not cut through both sides. Open it out a little and scrape out the seeds. Fill with one-sixth of the cheese mixture and secure with a cocktail stick. Continue to fill the remaining chillies in the same way. Put them on a greased baking tray and bake for about 10 minutes until the cheese is heated through. Remove the sticks and serve each chilli on a pool of warmed tomato sauce, topped with a sprig of coriander.

ARROZ ROJO
MEXICAN RED RICE

This is as much a staple side dish to Mexicans as potatoes are to us. Interestingly, potatoes are comparatively rare in Mexico, even though they come from the New World. Onions, garlic and tomatoes are the essential flavours here; peas are optional.

SERVES FOUR
AS A SIDE DISH
3 tbsp olive oil
1 onion, chopped
2 cloves garlic, chopped
1 jalapeño chilli, chopped
3 large tomatoes,
  roughly chopped
2 tsp tomato purée
220g white long-grain rice
550ml chicken or vegetable
  stock or water
60g peas, fresh or frozen
  (optional)
1 tsp salt (depending
  on saltiness of stock)
8 turns black peppermill
Small handful of
  coriander, chopped

Heat the oil in a saucepan and fry the onion, garlic and chilli over a medium heat for a few minutes until they're starting to soften but not brown. Add the tomatoes and tomato purée and stir for a couple of minutes.

Add the rice to the pan and stir to coat it in the tomato mixture. After a minute or so, add the stock and peas, if using, and season with salt and pepper. Put a lid on the pan and cook for 10–15 minutes until the rice has absorbed the liquid. Turn off the heat and allow the rice to rest for a few minutes. Fluff it up with a fork and serve sprinkled with chopped coriander.

TORTILLAS WITH BOILED EGGS & PUMPKIN SEED SAUCE

Don Hernan and his wife Azaria live in a traditional Mayan house in Santa Elena, near Mérida, with just one room, no windows and two doors, one facing east for the sunrise and the other west for the sunset. They are both in their seventies and have shared the same hammock all their married life. Their lifestyle is so simple, but it's hard to believe that they don't have a neat little bungalow somewhere nearby, because they have up to four tour groups visiting them every day, but they don't. They are devout Catholics but each day Don Hernan goes into his garden to a little table on which stand 10–15 tiny statues of Mayan gods and he prays and offers a drink of atole to them. It was a special moment; while I stood with him as he prayed and poured the atole on to the ground, a little breeze blew, just for a few seconds, then stopped. They were a lovely couple and Azaria cooked sikilpak sauce, which is delicious – a sort of Mexican version of hummus.

SERVES FOUR

12 x 15cm *Corn tortillas*
   (page 44 or bought)
8 hard-boiled eggs, peeled
   and roughly chopped
Extra herbs to garnish
   (optional)

For the sikilpak sauce
3 large ripe tomatoes
140g pumpkin seeds
½ tsp salt
Small handful of
   chives, chopped
Small handful of
   coriander, chopped

To make the sauce, roast the tomatoes in a dry heavy-based frying pan until they're charred and softened, then remove them and set them aside until cool enough to handle. In the same pan, roast the pumpkin seeds for a couple of minutes until you can smell their aroma and they puff up and pop in the pan. Don't let them burn. Remove the seeds from the pan and set aside a tablespoon for the garnish.

Peel the tomatoes and chop them roughly. Grind the pumpkin seeds in a spice or coffee grinder or a food processor until they resemble fine breadcrumbs. In a pestle and mortar or a separate bowl, crush the tomatoes and mash them to a lumpy pulp, then stir in the ground pumpkin seeds to form a loose sauce. Add the salt and chopped herbs and loosen the sauce with a little water if necessary to get a thick pouring consistency.

To serve, spread some of the sauce over the tortillas, top with chopped egg, then roll them up and eat just as they are. Alternatively, put the tortillas on plates, top with sauce and egg, then spoon over a little more of the sauce and garnish with the reserved pumpkin seeds and chopped herbs.

VERDURAS EN ESCABECHE
MEXICAN PICKLED VEGETABLES

Escabeche is a Mediterranean technique for preserving meat, fish or vegetables by part-cooking them, usually by frying, then putting them into a light vinegar pickle. The caramelisation effect of the frying imparts a special flavour. Mexican pickled vegetables are a very common accompaniment to meat tacos.

**MAKES ENOUGH
FOR A TWO-LITRE
KILNER JAR**

2 tbsp olive oil
3 carrots, sliced on
   the diagonal about
   5mm thick
150g cauliflower florets
4 green jalapeño
   chillies, whole
6 cloves garlic, peeled
1 onion, thickly sliced
400ml white wine
   or cider vinegar
1 tbsp brown sugar
1 bay leaf
6 peppercorns
4 allspice berries,
   bruised
1 tsp salt
2 small courgettes,
   cut on the diagonal into
   5mm slices
10 radishes, trimmed
   and cut in half
2 sprigs thyme

Heat the olive oil in a pan and sauté the carrots, cauliflower, jalapeños, garlic and onion for about 5 minutes. Add the vinegar, sugar, bay leaf, peppercorns, allspice berries, salt and 300ml of water and bring to the boil. Turn the heat down until the liquid is barely simmering and cook for another 5 minutes or so. The vegetables should still have some crunch.

Add the courgettes and radishes, then remove from the heat and leave the mixture to cool for 10 minutes. Transfer it to a sterilised Kilner jar and add the thyme sprigs. Seal the jar and once it is completely cold, put it in the fridge. Leave it for 3–5 days before serving with tacos, sandwiches and so on. This keeps for up to 3 weeks in the fridge.

ENSALADAS, VERDURAS Y GUARNICIONES
MEXICO
122

CHOPPED SALAD FROM LA SCALA

I'm a great fan of the chopped salad. It's all about the variety of the ingredients that you add and I like the way everything is a uniform size. And it's pleasingly American – like chopped liver, it says what it is. La Scala in Beverly Hills is said to have been the originator of the chopped salad. Gigi Leon, whose family has owned the restaurant since it opened in 1956, explained to me that it was exactly what the stars that frequent the restaurant need – something light, healthy and easy to eat. I recall explaining to her that for the same reason the Queen doesn't care for soup or pasta. What's needed is food that won't despoil a wonderful dress.

SERVES SIX
1 crisp iceberg lettuce,
    finely shredded
½ head romaine lettuce,
    finely shredded
120g Italian salami,
    cut into thin strips
    about 5cm long
200g fresh mozzarella,
    chopped
400g tin chickpeas,
    drained, rinsed and
    seasoned with ½ tsp salt
3 tomatoes, diced
15cm cucumber, diced
Small handful basil leaves,
    finely shredded

For the dressing
60ml olive oil
15ml red wine vinegar
½ tsp mustard powder
½ tsp salt
¼ tsp sugar
12 turns black peppermill

Mix the salad ingredients together in large bowl. Mix the dressing ingredients, add the dressing to the salad and toss well. Serve immediately.

CHAR-GRILLED AUBERGINE & FETA ROLLS

In Sausalito, just across the bay from San Francisco, there's an area filled with houseboats. They're beautiful, not boring little things, and some of them are permanently fixed on floating concrete pads. Others you can genuinely put to sea. Quite a few famous literary and arts figures have rented boats out there and invited friends like Jack Kerouac, Allen Ginsberg and William Burroughs to visit. And it is also where Otis Redding wrote 'Sittin' on the Dock of the Bay'. I was invited for lunch on a houseboat by Paula and Cory, whose best friend was English and had seen my programmes. In the end about 15 locals showed up, all bringing fabulous food. I know they may have been trying to impress, but they were all people who were used to cooking regularly and eating well and healthily. I remember thinking, this is California, this is good. These lovely aubergine rolls stuffed with feta were brought along by Olivia, one of the guests.

**SERVES FOUR
AS A STARTER OR
PART OF A MEZZE**

2 aubergines
4 tbsp olive oil
175g feta cheese
175g ricotta cheese
Small handful flatleaf
  parsley, chopped
5–6 rasps freshly
  grated nutmeg
10 turns black peppermill
1½ tbsp capers, chopped

To serve
100g mixed rocket,
  watercress and
  baby spinach
Juice of ½ lemon
2 tbsp extra virgin olive oil
Seeds from ½ pomegranate
Salt and pepper

Cut the aubergines lengthwise into slices about 5mm thick. You should get about 6 slices from each aubergine. Brush the aubergine slices on both sides with oil and grill them in batches on a barbecue or griddle pan for 3–4 minutes on each side until browned, tender and pliable. Set them aside.

Mash the feta and ricotta in a bowl with a fork and add the parsley, nutmeg and black pepper. Stir in the capers.

Spoon a generous tablespoon of filling on to the wide end of each aubergine slice and roll it up like a Swiss roll.

To serve, arrange the salad leaves on a platter, dress them with lemon juice and olive oil, then season. Arrange the aubergine rolls on top, seam-side down, and decorate them with pomegranate seeds. Serve at room temperature as a starter or part of a mezze.

COURGETTE SALAD

Chef Miguel Angel Guerrero's restaurant La Esperanza BajaMed is the most highly regarded in the Guadelupe Valley. He lives just outside Tijuana at Rosarito. What endeared me to Miguel was his enormous pride in his really rather spectacular kitchen garden, which he genuinely uses to supply his restaurants. He's a very charismatic character and the inventor of BajaMed cuisine which celebrates local ingredients with a nod to the Mediterranean, as the climate and terroir are similar. This is a typical example – capers and olive oil from the Med; chilli and pumpkin seeds from Baja. He's a great modern Mexican cook. There's another of his recipes on page 253.

SERVES FOUR

4 medium-sized green
   or yellow courgettes
100ml olive oil
2 cloves garlic, finely sliced
20g capers, drained
A good pinch of thyme leaves
A good pinch of chilli flakes

For the dressing
1 tbsp pumpkin seeds
4 tbsp olive oil
1 tbsp chopped parsley
1 tbsp lemon juice
1 tsp dried seaweed flakes
½ tsp salt

Slice the courgettes very thinly on a mandolin or with a potato peeler. Arrange the courgette slices on a platter. Heat the olive oil in a small saucepan and gently fry the garlic, capers, thyme and chilli flakes until fragrant and golden but not burnt.

In a separate dry pan, fry the pumpkin seeds for the dressing until they pop, then set them aside. Add a tablespoon of the oil to the pan and fry the parsley very briefly.

Pour the fried ingredients over the courgette slices and dress with the remaining olive oil, lemon juice, pumpkin seeds, seaweed flakes and salt.

THE ORIGINAL CAESAR SALAD

The original is not always better than the derivatives, but I'm pleased to report that this is the case with Caesar salad. This is the recipe from Caesar's Hotel in Tijuana, where it was created. It benefits enormously from being simple. I'm almost fanatical about the fact that it must be made with salted anchovies, not the pickled white variety. The waiters, many of whom look like they've been there since the earliest days of the restaurant in the 1920s, make the salad for you at the table. I remarked to the owner Javier Plascencia that the return of such table theatre dishes, like crêpes suzette and steak Diane, are long overdue and he was much in agreement. His family and other restaurants in the area have been largely responsible for making Tijuana such a rejuvenated city.

SERVES TWO

4 slices of baguette,
   brushed with olive oil
1 large head of
   romaine lettuce
150ml extra virgin olive oil
1 tsp Worcestershire sauce
¾ tsp Dijon mustard
6 salted anchovy fillets,
   mashed in a pestle
   and mortar
Juice of 1 lime
1 clove garlic, crushed
30g Parmesan cheese,
   freshly grated
1 egg, room temperature
8 turns black peppermill

Preheat the oven to 180°C/Fan 160°C and bake the baguette slices for 5–6 minutes until crisp and golden. Wash and dry the lettuce and keep it in the fridge until the last minute so it stays crisp.

In a roomy bowl, combine the olive oil, Worcestershire sauce, mustard, anchovies, lime juice, garlic and half of the grated Parmesan. Beat with a balloon whisk until the mixture forms a paste.

Bring a small pan of water to the boil, add the whole egg in its shell and cook it for exactly one minute. Crack the egg into the dressing and whisk until thoroughly blended, then add the whole lettuce leaves and coat them in the dressing.

Serve the salad on a platter, season with black pepper and top with the remaining grated Parmesan and baguette croutons.

PERSIAN FRITTATA

Samin Nosrat lives in San Francisco and trained at Chez Panisse. She is, I suspect, about to become very well known in the UK with her book *Salt, Fat, Acid, Heat: Mastering the Elements of Good Cooking*. While waiting to film her making this dish, I picked up a copy of the book and was instantly captivated because it's about learning to cook instinctively. So often when someone says they can't cook you feel like telling them – just trust your taste. A lot of people simply don't taste as they cook, which would be anathema to Samin. This wonderful Persian frittata says it all. *Recipe photograph overleaf*

**SERVES SIX
TO EIGHT**

400g green chard
300g spinach
1 large leek, trimmed
5 tbsp olive oil
2 bulbs spring 'wet' garlic,
   or 1 large clove of garlic,
   sliced or 2 handfuls of
   wild garlic leaves
20g mint, chopped
20g basil, chopped
100g coriander leaves
   and stems, chopped
9 eggs
1½ tsp salt
12 turns black peppermill
45g unsalted butter

For the side salad
1 cucumber, finely sliced
200g radishes, trimmed
   and finely sliced
15g mint, roughly chopped
15g basil, roughly chopped
120g feta cheese, crumbled

For the dressing
1 tsp coriander seeds
2 bulbs spring 'wet' garlic,
   or 1 large clove garlic,
   sliced
¼ tsp salt
4 tbsp extra virgin olive oil
1½ tbsp lemon juice

Wash the chard, strip out the stems and chop them, then roughly chop the leaves. Wash the spinach, then roughly chop the leaves. Cut the leek into quarters lengthwise and then into 1cm slices. Wash the slices well.

Heat 4 tablespoons of the oil in a frying pan. Add the chard stems, leeks and whichever garlic you're using and sweat gently for 15–20 minutes until soft. Set aside.

Put the spinach and chard leaves in a separate pan with the water that clings to them after washing and wilt for 3–5 minutes until soft. Drain them in a colander and when cool enough to handle squeeze them into a ball, chop and set aside in a large bowl. Add the chopped herbs, then the sweated leeks and garlic. Break the eggs into the bowl, mix well and season with salt and black pepper. Preheat the oven to 175°C/Fan 155°C.

Add the remaining oil and the butter to a 25–30cm ovenproof non-stick frying pan or a casserole dish. Pour in the egg mixture and cook it over a very low heat for about 10 minutes until set. Use a spatula to check the bottom is golden brown. Transfer the pan to the oven and cook for a further 10–15 minutes until the top is cooked and firm. Place a baking sheet on top of the pan, then flip the frittata upside down and slide it on to a plate. Serve it warm, at room temperature or cold with the salad.

For the salad, mix the cucumber, radishes and herbs in a bowl, then sprinkle with the feta. Crush the coriander seeds in a pestle and mortar, then mix in the spring garlic or garlic clove and the salt. Add the oil and lemon juice and toss well.

ENSALADAS, VERDURAS Y GUARNICIONES
SAN FRANCISCO

THE HITCHING POST'S GLOBE ARTICHOKES WITH CHIPOTLE MAYO

The Hitching Post II is just outside Buellton near Santa Barbara, California. Frankly the reason for going there was that the bar features prominently in a favourite film of mine, *Sideways*. I just had to have steak grilled over oakwood and drink a glass of their Pinot Noir Highliner 2014, just like Miles Raymond, played by Paul Giamatti in the film.

It proved to be quite as good as promised, both steak and wine, and the owner and producer of the wine, Frank Ostini, was a man after my own heart. He doesn't actually own a vineyard or a winery but produces his excellent reds in a production unit shared by about ten other winemakers nearby. There is not a lot of point in doing a recipe for the steak because you need California oak plus a Santa Maria grill. This is modelled on the barbecues you see in the Basque country of northern Spain, which can be raised and lowered above the fire by a handle, giving perfect control of the heat. However, the accompaniment that I really rated was this grilled artichoke dish. I have slightly changed the sauce and not grilled the artichokes but tossed them in butter and white wine instead, and it's great with a steak or as a first course.

SERVES FOUR

4 globe artichokes
½ lemon
Salt
2 tbsp butter, melted
2 tbsp olive oil
2 tbsp dry white wine
2 tbsp lemon juice
Freshly ground black pepper

For the chipotle mayonnaise
150ml mayonnaise
3 tbsp *Chipotles en adobo*
   (page 298 or bought)

Break off the tough outer leaves of each artichoke, cut off the top third with a knife and cut the stalk close to the base. Wash the artichokes with cold water. Bring a pan of water to the boil with the juice of the lemon half (throw the lemon in as well) and a teaspoon of salt per 600ml of water. When the water is boiling, add the artichokes and cook until they are tender and the base offers no resistance when pierced with a knife. This will take 30–45 minutes depending upon size. Allow them to cool.

Cut the artichokes into quarters and remove the hairy choke inside each one with a teaspoon and discard. Mix the mayonnaise with the chipotles en adobo and set aside in a small serving bowl.

Heat the butter and olive oil in a large frying pan and add the artichoke quarters. Add the white wine and lemon juice and baste the artichokes while they cook for 3–4 minutes. Season with salt and pepper and serve with the spicy chipotle mayonnaise.

CAULIFLOWER FRITTERS WITH CASHEW SAUCE

This recipe comes from a vegan restaurant called Gracias Madre on Melrose Avenue, West Hollywood. The owners' son Ryland Engelhart explained to me how his parents, Matthew and Terces, had taught him and his sister about the true meaning of the word passion. In their view it is 'found among individuals whose love for what they do is not a facade but an extension of a dream founded long ago, an opportunity to turn their vision for food and people into a franchise built on one unifying thread – love, a love for the process that goes into food'. This might seem a little tiresomely solemn, but having spoken to him, I'm not so sure. There is thinking in California that much of what we have become used to eating is bad for us, bad for animals and bad for the planet. The fact is that this restaurant attracts every well-known film star, director and personality around and they are doing really good business. This cauliflower dish is just a small part of the careful vegan food they sell.

SERVES FOUR

1 large cauliflower,
  cut into florets
750ml corn oil, for frying
Lemon wedges, to serve

For the sauce
300g cashew nuts
60g pumpkin seeds
1 clove garlic, chopped
1 jalapeño pepper,
  roughly chopped
1 tsp salt
Juice of a lemon
1 tsp smoked paprika

Start by making the sauce. Soak the cashew nuts in 400ml water for a couple of hours. Toast the pumpkin seeds in a dry frying pan until they start to pop. Put the cashew nuts and their soaking water into a blender with the garlic, jalapeño, 50g of the pumpkin seeds, salt, lemon juice and paprika and whizz to make a thick sauce.

Heat the oil to 180°C in a large saucepan and fry the cauliflower florets until golden and crispy. Drain them on kitchen paper. Toss them in the sauce, garnish with the remaining pumpkin seeds and serve with lemon wedges.

BURRATA WITH SPECK & PEAS

This recipe comes from Osteria Mozza, another very successful restaurant on Melrose Avenue, Los Angeles. The chef and owner Nancy Silverton, while famous throughout the United States, initially for her fantastic sourdoughs, still finds time to conduct the operation of the mozzarella bar, which is the heart of the restaurant. It involves creating endless light and delicate first courses from cheeses such as mozzarella and burrata. Her idea entirely suits the zeitgeist of LA – healthy, a little rich but in no way challenging to the figure. This is what Nancy prepared for me but she could have done ten different versions without drawing breath. I thought it was a brilliant idea. *Recipe photograph overleaf*

**SERVES FOUR
AS A STARTER**

500g fresh peas in pods
  (about 250g shelled
  weight)
20 sugar snap peas
20 mint leaves
3 tbsp freshly grated
  Parmesan, plus extra
  for serving
2 tbsp extra virgin olive oil
16 slices speck or prosciutto
225g burrata
Salt and pepper

Shell the peas and cook them in salted boiling water for about 1½ minutes until bright green but still with a little bite to them. Drain them immediately and refresh them under very cold running water until cold. Drain well on kitchen paper.

Slice the sugar snap peas on the diagonal into really long strips, about 3mm thick. Put the peas, sugar snap strips and mint in a bowl and add the Parmesan and olive oil. Season with salt and pepper.

Arrange some speck slices like a rose in the centre of each plate. Cut the burrata into 4 segments and nestle one in the centre of each portion of ham. Pile the peas and sugar snap strips on top of the burrata and grate over a little extra Parmesan.

RICOTTA DUMPLINGS WITH CHILLI BUTTER SAUCE

Francisco (Paco) Ruano is the chef at Alcalde in Guadalajara. It's probably the smartest place in the city and one of the top 50 best restaurants in Latin America. Paco is one of the celebrated new breed of Mexican chefs, and this is his recipe, light and delicate but still recognisably Mexican.

SERVES EIGHT

For the dumplings
125g maize tortilla flour
½ tsp salt
175–180ml water
15g butter, melted
2 tbsp milk
125g ricotta cheese

For the spinach
15g butter
1 onion, finely chopped
2 cloves garlic, finely chopped
300g spinach, washed and
    dried, shredded
2 tomatoes, finely chopped
Juice of ½ lemon
½ tsp salt

For the chilli butter sauce
3 poblano chillies, or 3
    romano or green peppers,
    deseeded and sliced
1 green jalapeño chilli
    (seeds in), roughly chopped
50g butter
200ml chicken or
    vegetable stock
30g maize tortilla flour
2–3 tbsp double cream
Juice of ½ lemon

To serve
30g macadamia nuts, toasted
    and ground to a powder
1 tbsp chopped coriander

Mix the dumpling ingredients in a food processor and pulse to bring them together into a dough. Spoon the mixture on to squares of cling film, shape into golfball-sized dumplings and twist the cling film to tie them up – you should get 8 dumplings. Bring a pan of water to the boil, add the dumplings, then turn the heat down and poach them for 20–30 minutes.

For the spinach, melt the butter in a pan, add the onion and garlic and sweat them for 5 minutes or so until softened. Add the spinach and fry until the liquid from the spinach has reduced down. Add the chopped tomatoes and season with lemon juice and salt. Cook for 3–4 minutes to bring everything together, then remove the pan from the heat and set aside to keep warm.

For the sauce, sweat the chillies in the butter until soft. Put them in a blender with the stock and whizz until smooth, then pour the mixture into a saucepan. Add the flour to thicken and whisk until smooth, then add the double cream and lemon juice.

Spoon some of the spinach mixture into each serving bowl. Unwrap a dumpling or two and place them on top, then spoon over some of the chilli butter sauce. Garnish with the ground macadamia nuts and coriander.

PESCADOS y MARISCOS

FISH & SHELLFISH

We had been told that the fishermen would be back in ten minutes. The first thing they'd do would be to make a fish stew for their supper on the beach by their thatched shed and they would be very hungry. We stood around on the scruffy beach and waited. A few dogs waited too, standing by the old freezer chests on their sides, some with panels missing showing the brown insulation, all smelling of old fish. We waited by piles of old nets tangled with dried seaweed and by old pipes and pieces of sun-dried flotsam from the tide. We joked about never catching any fish when we go filming with fishermen at sea and now there aren't even any fishermen.

Then our contact, Ramon, pointed to a couple of tiny dots on the horizon and they swept in, a couple of sun-bleached, ugly-looking boats, like floating fish boxes and green with weed but with big onboard motors and just the word 'Campeche' stencilled on them. They landed a couple of boxes of small fish, mostly bream. They built a small fire of bone-dry driftwood in the shelter of an upturned dingy and put a rusty grill bar on the top and a thin aluminium pot, which they filled with fresh water. They added a lid with no handle on top and waited for the water to boil. Using the top of a red insulated food box as a work surface, one of them chopped onions, garlic, green chillies and coriander. Another sliced up a few of the fish and dropped them into the now boiling water. They added tomatoes, pepper and salt, then everything else except some of the chopped onions and chillies and coriander which they sprinkled over their fish caldo as they served it. With simple ingredients and the freshest of fish, this was remarkably good, especially with the addition of onions, chillies and coriander, plus a squeeze of lime juice.

Needless to say, California and Mexico have so much coastline that the seafood alone is good reason for going there. Perhaps the most common dish everywhere is ceviche (page 164), which is so special in Mexico. I think it's something to do with the limes there – they are ever so slightly sweeter than ours. I have to say, though, if you make no other dish in this book try the prawn panuchos, again from Campeche, on page 158. This was one of the most repeatedly requested dishes by all of the film crew.

SOPA DE MARISCOS
A SEAFOOD STEW WITH JALAPEÑO & GUAJILLO

There are more recipes for sopa de mariscos than you can shake a stick at, and many are absurdly complicated. I was extremely keen on this one from El Camello restaurant in Tulum, Yucatán – the name 'camel' is the nickname of the owner. I was immediately taken with the restaurant as I used to play for the Wadebridge Camels, my local rugby club, in the 70s and still keep in touch. And I like anything named after that beast. I asked for the recipe and got a typical chef's version with a few lines saying something along these lines.

'Make a tomato sauce with lots of guajillo chillies. Make a good prawn and fish stock, fry some onions, peppers and jalapeño. Put everything together, simmer a bit, then add prawns, crab meat and squid.' Actually, rather than jalapeños, they used a yellow xcactic chilli which is very local and not likely to appear in my neck of the woods anytime soon.

SERVES FOUR TO SIX

80ml corn oil
2 onions, chopped
4 cloves garlic, chopped
3 guajillo chillies, sliced
350g tomatoes, chopped
1 tbsp tomato purée
1 tsp oregano
2 tsp salt
1 red pepper deseeded, and roughly chopped
2 jalapeño chillies, sliced
800ml *Fish stock* (page 300)
800ml *Shellfish stock* (page 300)
2 tsp dried epazote (optional) or oregano
150g squid sliced into rings
150g cooked, peeled prawns
120g crab meat
Small handful coriander, roughly chopped

Heat half the corn oil in a pan and fry half of the onions with the garlic and guajillo chillies until soft. Add the tomatoes, tomato purée, oregano, salt and 300ml of water and cook down to thickish paste. Tip it all into a blender and liquidise, then set aside.

Heat the rest of the oil in the pan and fry the red pepper and jalapeños with the rest of the onion until soft, then set aside.

Put the fish and shellfish stocks in a saucepan with the tomato and guajillo sauce and bring to the boil. Simmer for 20 minutes, adding the epazote or oregano for the last couple of minutes.

Add the squid and the red pepper mixture, then cook for a couple of minutes. Add the prawns and crab and warm through. Ladle the soup into deep bowls, sprinkle with coriander and serve with a pile of tortillas or crusty bread.

MOJARRA A LA DIABLA
DEEP-FRIED BREAM WITH HOT SALSA

I'm endlessly surprised by the fact that many viewers of the TV series that accompany my books like *The Road to Mexico* want to go to all the tiny places I visited. This might include a long journey into the Chinantlan Mountains in the state of Oaxaca. The journey to San Mateo Yetla from the city of Oaxaca takes eight hours using good roads or, though far shorter distance-wise, twelve hours using mountain roads. There you will find some very special cabins. Don't expect an Aman resort – it's extremely basic. You could almost call it camping. But you're by a clear mountain river, the water of which is diverted off into a swimming pool. For breakfast they'll give you café de olla, mountain coffee served in vast terracotta bowls with no handles. Later you'll eat fried mojarra fish and freshwater prawns from the river. The fish is served basted with a searingly hot tomato and chilli sauce containing three types – chiles de árbol, guajillo and chipotle. I was completely captivated, not only by the fish but also by the fact that we shared a couple of bottles of 3V Cabernet Sauvignon from the Casa Madero winery in the northeastern state of Coahuila. I've written this recipe for fillets rather than for the whole, rather bony, fish.

SERVES TWO

3 guajillo chillies,
　seeds shaken out
1 ½ tbsp olive oil
4–5 chiles de árbol,
　depending on how
　hot you want to go
½ small onion,
　roughly chopped
2 cloves garlic, halved
2 tbsp *Chipotles en adobo*
　(page 298 or bought)
2 tomatoes, halved
3 tbsp mayonnaise
½ tsp salt
1 litre corn oil
600g sea bream, filleted
4–5 tbsp maize
　tortilla flour
Sliced avocado, to serve

Soak the guajillo chillies in 250ml of just-boiled water for 20 minutes, then drain them. Heat the olive oil in a frying pan and fry the chiles de árbol, onion and garlic. When they're softened, put them in a blender or food processor with the drained guajillos, the chipotles en adobo, tomatoes, mayonnaise and 75ml of water and blend to a smooth sauce. Transfer the sauce to a pan and heat it through for 5 minutes until it turns a deep red colour. Add the salt.

In a frying pan, heat the corn oil to 185°C. Dredge the fish fillets in maize flour and fry them for 3–4 minutes until crisp and golden. Drain the fish on kitchen paper.

Brush the fillets on both sides with some of the sauce and serve with sliced avocado and a side salad.

SPLASH CAFÉ CLAM CHOWDER IN SOURDOUGH BOWLS

Chowders served in the way the French call 'en croustade' are a bit of a speciality in California, though this white chowder would have originated in New England. The idea for this dish came from the Splash Café in Pismo Beach whose motto is 'clam capital of the world'. The owner Joanne Currie wouldn't give me the recipe. I don't blame her. Any place with just one famous product needs to keep their recipe secret, and famous it is. They make over 40,000 gallons of chowder each year from their two really quite small restaurants. Never mind, I have written a few recipes for chowder in my time and as I'm not in the clam capital of the world I have made this with some white fish as well, as otherwise it takes a lot of clams. I liked Joanne because I was able to share some thoughts about how hard you have to work to make restaurants successful. *Recipe photograph overleaf*

SERVES SIX

6 sourdough bread
   rolls or crusty rolls
   (about 12cm diameter)
1kg fresh clams, scrubbed
225g waxy potatoes, peeled
40g unsalted butter
75g smoked streaky
   bacon, chopped
1 small onion or banana
   shallot, finely chopped
1 leek, cleaned, halved
   lengthways and
   finely chopped
2 sticks celery, chopped
30g plain flour
500ml whole milk
200ml double cream
1 bay leaf
200g cod fillet (or other
   white fish), skinned
   and cut into 2cm pieces
1 tsp salt
10 turns black peppermill
A few rasps freshly
   grated nutmeg
Small handful flatleaf
   parsley or chives,
   chopped

Cut the tops off the rolls and scoop out as much of the dough as you can, leaving the crust.

Heat 250ml of water in a large shallow pan and add the clams. Put a lid on the pan and allow the clams to steam for 3–4 minutes until they open. Set a colander over a bowl, drain the opened clams and reserve the cooking liquid. When the clams are cool enough to handle, remove the meat from the shells and set aside.

Cut the potatoes into 1.5cm dice and boil them for 5–10 minutes until tender, then drain and set aside.

Melt the butter in a separate large pan over a medium heat and fry the bacon, onion or shallot, leek and celery until soft. Add the plain flour and cook for a minute or so, then add the reserved clam cooking liquor and stir until thickened. Add the milk, cream, bay leaf, potatoes and cod, then bring to the boil. Turn the heat down and simmer for about 5 minutes until the cod is cooked, then add the clam meat and season with salt, pepper and nutmeg.

Spoon the chowder into the hollowed-out bread rolls or serve in bowls with sourdough on the side. Garnish the chowder with chopped parsley or chives.

CALDO DE PESCADO

FISHERMAN'S CALDO FROM CAMPECHE

This is a very simple fisherman's soup, just as they make it on the boat with a few simple ingredients and fish straight from the sea. The freshness of the fish and the punchy kick of the limey, spicy, salty, onion salsa are what make the stew sing.

SERVES FOUR TO SIX AS A STARTER

2 tbsp olive oil
1 onion, chopped
1 green pepper,
   deseeded and chopped
2 cloves garlic,
   finely chopped
4 ripe tomatoes, chopped
1 tsp salt
15 turns black peppermill
350g very fresh whole
   white fish fillets such as
   whiting, pollock or bream
Handful coriander, chopped
1 lime cut into wedges,
   to serve

For the salsa
1 onion, sliced
Juice of 2 limes
1 tsp salt
1 habanero chilli,
   finely chopped

Heat the olive oil in a large pan and fry the onion and pepper until they start to soften. Add the garlic and tomatoes and fry for another 2 minutes, then season with salt and pepper and add a litre of water. Put a lid on the pan and cook for 20 minutes. Then add the fish fillets and coriander and continue to cook for 5 minutes while you make the salsa.

For the salsa, mix the onion with the lime juice, salt and habanero, then set aside.

Ladle the soup into warmed bowls and serve the salsa and lime wedges separately at the table so everyone can help themselves.

PRAWN PANUCHOS WITH AVOCADO & REFRIED BEANS

I often talk to people about the places where we've been filming and if they know the city, they will usually say, 'Did you stay at?' Then mention one of the most expensive hotels. I always reply: 'TV budget'. But in Mexico I found that just because a hotel was cheaper never meant that the food wasn't as good as anywhere else. And the prawn panuchos at the Holiday Inn in Campeche were a case in point. They were just a few small tortillas, deep-fried and filled with refried beans, fried chopped prawns, tomato sauce and shredded lettuce and none of us could get enough of them. One night I said, 'I'll just have two helpings of panuchos, please.'

SERVES FOUR (MAKES TWELVE PANUCHOS)

For the tomato sauce
1 tbsp olive oil
1 garlic clove, chopped
2 ripe red tomatoes, chopped
1 onion, chopped
1 red chilli, finely chopped
½ tsp salt
10 turns black peppermill

For the panuchos
1 quantity *Corn tortilla dough* (page 44) or use bought 10cm tacos
750ml corn or vegetable oil, for frying

For the prawns
2 tbsp olive oil
1 onion, chopped
1 tomato, chopped
225g raw peeled prawns, chopped
½ tsp dried oregano
1 bay leaf, torn

To serve
Refried beans (page 104)
1 little gem lettuce, shredded
Pink pickled onions (page 296)
1 large avocado, stoned, peeled and sliced

For the tomato sauce, heat the olive oil in a frying pan and add the garlic, tomatoes, onion and the chilli. Season with salt and pepper and sauté until the ingredients are softened and slightly browned. Tip everything into a pestle and mortar and pound to a smooth sauce, or pulse in a food processor or blender. Taste and adjust the seasoning if necessary, then set the sauce aside.

Roll or press the dough into 12 rounds, each about 8cm in diameter and 2–3mm thick. Heat the corn or vegetable oil in a saucepan to 190°C and fry the rounds, a few at a time, for 2–3 minutes until puffed up. Remove them from the oil and drain on kitchen paper. Keep them warm while you finish the toppings.

For the prawns, heat the oil in a frying pan and add the chopped onion. After 2 minutes, once it has softened, add the tomato and cook for a minute or two until it's starting to break down. Add the chopped prawns, oregano and bay leaf.

Warm the refried beans in a separate pan. Flatten down the centres of the puffed-up panuchos with the back of a spoon and spread them with some of the refried beans. Set 3 panuchos on each plate and top with some of the fried prawn mixture, shredded lettuce, pink pickled onions and a slice of avocado. Serve the tomato sauce on the side.

DEEP-FRIED COCONUT PRAWNS

If you have been anywhere by the sea in the Yucatán peninsula you will have had these deep-fried king prawns with a coconut batter. Somewhat curiously to me, they often come with an apple sauce, but far less frequently they're served with a papaya and habanero dipping sauce, which I like. The other problem is the batter is often too sweet, so this is my version with no sugar. The sauce is a little on the hot side, but so it should be, habaneros being far and away the chillies most often used in the Yucatán.

SERVES FOUR TO SIX AS A STARTER
24 raw king prawns, peeled but with tails on (about 600g frozen raw shell-on prawns)
600ml corn oil, for frying
Salt and black pepper

For the batter
125g plain flour
1½ tsp baking powder
1 tsp salt
1 medium egg
150ml ice-cold water

For coating
50g plain flour
60g panko breadcrumbs
60g unsweetened desiccated coconut

For the papaya dipping sauce
1 large papaya
½–1 habanero chilli, stem removed, deseeded and roughly chopped
1 banana shallot, roughly chopped
1 clove garlic, peeled and halved
3 tbsp cider vinegar
2 thin slices root ginger
Juice of 1 lime
Juice of 1 orange
1 tbsp soft brown sugar
1 large pinch ground allspice
½ tsp salt

To make the dipping sauce, peel the papaya, remove the seeds and chop it roughly. Put it in a blender with the other ingredients and process until smooth. Pour the sauce into a pan and bring it to the boil, then immediately turn down to a simmer and cook gently for about 5 minutes. If the sauce gets too thick, add a few tablespoons of just-boiled water.

For the batter, sift the plain flour, baking powder and salt into a bowl. Make a well in centre and break in the egg, then bring in the flour from the sides. Whisk in the cold water to make a smooth batter.

Put the coating flour in a shallow bowl. Put the batter in a second bowl and the breadcrumbs mixed with coconut in a third.

Season the prawns with salt and pepper, then coat a prawn in flour, shaking off any excess and holding it by the tail, dip it into the batter. Lift it out and let any excess batter drip back into the bowl. Roll the prawn in the crumbs and coconut mix, pressing it down so the mixture sticks. Put the prawn on a plate lined with greaseproof paper and repeat until all are coated. Leave some space between each one.

Add the oil to a large pan and heat to 180°C. Deep-fry the prawns – a few at a time – for 1 or 2 minutes until golden and crisp. Drain them on kitchen paper. Serve at once with the papaya dipping sauce.

ABRAHAM'S CEVICHE OF BASS & PRAWNS WITH CHILLI

Abraham is a fisherman who took me and Jeremiah Tower out early one morning from Progreso, which is about 45 minutes from Mérida. He says that when making ceviche you should only leave the fish in the lime juice for the time it takes to prepare the other ingredients. This interested me because Laura, the Peruvian restaurant manager at our café, says we don't know how to make proper ceviche in the UK. She puts it down to the limes, which are different, and I can understand that now if Peruvian limes are similar to the Mexican ones, which confusingly they call limón and are sweeter and less harsh than ours. I agree, though, that the other mistake we tend to make is leaving the fish in the lime juice too long. Abraham and his young apprentice filleted fish, which were mostly a type of bream, on board the boat and made the ceviche. I have a wonderful photo of Jeremiah carrying the bowl with much reverence to where we were going to eat on the shore. You can make the classic version, but for the restaurant we add prawns for sweetness and avocado for a little richness.

SERVES SIX AS A STARTER

500g very fresh bass or bream fillets
80g cooked, peeled prawns (optional)
125ml freshly squeezed lime juice (3–4 limes)
½–1 tsp fine salt
1 banana shallot
½–1 red habanero, deseeded
Handful fresh coriander
2 large ripe tomatoes
1 small avocado, stoned and peeled (optional)
Totopos (page 299), to serve

Skin the fish fillets and cut them into 1cm pieces. Mix the fish and the prawns, if using, with the lime juice and salt and leave them for a few minutes while you prepare the remaining ingredients.

Finely chop the shallot and the habanero, then chop the coriander and tomatoes and dice the avocado, if using. Combine the fish with the other ingredients and serve immediately with totopos.

FISH PIBIL WITH CHILLIES & ACHIOTE

As I have mentioned elsewhere a pibil, meat wrapped in banana leaves and cooked in a pit, is a method of cooking used all over Mexico but particularly in Yucatán with its pre-Hispanic Mayan origins. A fish pibil is unusual but I was very taken with the flavours and satisfying strangeness of achiote paste with really good fish. It goes without saying that this must be served with hot corn tortillas, and while you might find the squirting of mayo on the fish just before baking a bit out of place, it works and gives the dish a very enticing creaminess. I have modified this recipe so it can be baked in your oven.

SERVES SIX

Corn oil
1 large onion, sliced
1 green pepper, sliced
3 green serrano or jalapeño chillies, sliced
6 tomatoes, sliced
2 tbsp corn oil
4 cloves garlic, chopped
30g achiote paste
1½ tsp salt
8 turns black peppermill
100ml orange juice (preferably from Seville oranges)
1 x 1.5kg grey mullet, cleaned and whole
4 tbsp mayonnaise (Kewpie in a squeezy bottle is best for this)

Preheat the oven to 200°C/Fan 180°C. Oil a large oven dish and add the slices of onion, pepper, chillies and tomatoes. Drizzle over a tablespoon of corn oil and roast the vegetables in the oven for 20 minutes. Heat another tablespoon of oil in a small pan and sweat the garlic until soft.

Mash the achiote paste in a pestle and mortar, add the salt, pepper, orange juice and cooked garlic and pound everything well to make a marinade. Alternatively, you can mix the achiote and other ingredients in a blender.

Place the fish on the vegetables, moving a few of them on top of the fish, then pour over the marinade, and drizzle with the mayonnaise. Cover the dish with foil to seal the moisture in. Bake in the oven for about 50 minutes until the fish is cooked. You can check it with a probe if you have one. When the internal temperature reaches 65°C, the fish should be done.

GRILLED MACKEREL & RADISHES WITH A MANDARIN & HERB SALAD

Trying to get a table at Hartwood, Eric Werner's fascinating restaurant on the beach at Tulum, is very hard indeed. I could easily understand why: the restaurant is about as sustainable in energy use and care of the environment as you can get, the biodegradable nature of his kitchen and toilets is a scientific marvel, and Eric himself is a delight. Originally he cooked in several famous NY restaurants and he's young, handsome and incredibly charismatic. It sort of feels like Chez Panisse in its very early days. I met Eric on the beach earlier that morning, buying small grey mullet from a local fisherman. He grilled them over hardwood, but I know he would have treated any small fresh fish in the same way, so I've no doubt that if he were in Cornwall and there were some nice fat mackerel being landed, that's what he'd use.

SERVES TWO

2 fresh mackerel,
    butterflied (page 308)
½ white radish (mooli),
    sliced lengthways
    into 3mm thick slices
Pinch salt
8 turns black peppermill
½ orange cut into wedges
Tajín seasoning

For the gaujillo oil
200ml corn or olive oil
2 guajillo chillies, chopped

For the salad
A couple of handfuls of
    interesting leaves and
    herbs such as wild garlic,
    sorrel, basil, mint, parsley,
    little gem lettuce
1 mandarin, peeled
    and segmented

For the salad dressing
30ml olive oil
2 tsp lime juice
1 tsp honey
¼ tsp salt

First prepare the guajillo oil. Heat 2 tablespoons of the oil in a pan and fry the chillies for 2 minutes. Add the remaining oil and warm for 4–5 minutes. Let the oil cool, then pour it into a sterilised jam jar or wide-necked bottle and use it as required.

Heat up your barbecue and preheat the oven to 120°C/Fan 100°C. Season the mackerel and the white radish slices with salt and pepper, then grill them on the barbecue in a fish clamp for about 4 minutes on each side. Transfer them to the oven to keep warm while you prepare the salad and mix the ingredients for the dressing.

Drizzle the fish and white radish with the guajillo oil and serve with the dressed salad and the orange wedges dipped in the Tajín seasoning mix.

BUTTERFLIED GRILLED BASS WITH GREEN & RED SALSAS

This recipe comes from a very good seafood restaurant called Contramar, which is in Roma (Mexico City). The pleasing realisation comes to most people after a few days in El D.F (as the locals call their city) that it is not one massive jam of traffic, smog and danger. There are parts where you could be in Barcelona or Madrid, and Roma has some beautiful tree-lined streets with fabulously ornate apartment blocks in typically Mexican pinks, blues and oranges. Contramar is typical of the area – very trendy and with queues always. You've got to love this dish, which is a butterflied fish with salsa verde on one side and salsa rojo on the other. If served on a white plate it makes the Mexican flag, less the plumed serpent in the middle.

SERVES TWO

2 whole bass, each about
  350g, gutted and
  butterflied (page 308)

Salsa verde (green sauce)
Handful each of
  coriander and chives
2 cloves garlic,
  peeled and sliced
100–120ml olive oil
¼ tsp salt
1 tsp lime juice
1 serrano chilli, sliced

Chile rojo (red sauce)
3 dried guajillo chillies
  and 2 ancho chillies,
  stems removed,
  seeds shaken out
1 medium tomato
1 tbsp olive oil
½ small onion, chopped
2 cloves garlic, chopped
½ tsp dried oregano
¼ tsp ground cumin
¼ – ½ tsp salt

To serve
1 tbsp soured cream
1 tbsp mayonnaise
1 tbsp salsa verde
Squeeze of lime juice
Refried beans (page 104)

To make the salsa verde, put the ingredients, starting with 100ml of the oil, in a blender. Blend to a smooth sauce, then add more oil if necessary to loosen the mixture.

For the chili rojo, toast the chillies in a hot dry frying pan. Take care not to burn them. Put them in a bowl with 300ml of just-boiled water and leave to soften 20 minutes. In the frying pan, char the tomato on all sides until it starts to soften, then cut it into quarters. Add the oil to the pan and fry the onion and garlic until softened. Add the tomato, drained softened chillies, the oregano and cumin and cook for about 5 minutes.

Put the tomato and onion mixture in a blender with 75–100ml of the chilli soaking liquid. Season with salt and blend until smooth.

Preheat your grill. Coat one fillet with some salsa verde and the other with salsa rojo. Grill for 5 minutes or until the internal temperature reaches 60–62°C. Mix the soured cream with the mayo, a tablespoon of salsa verde and a squeeze of lime juice. Serve alongside the fish with some refried beans.

SIR FRANCIS SQUID WITH ALMONDS, GUAJILLO CHILLI & POTATOES

Carlos Acosta was one of the most congenial chefs I met on my whole journey and La Pigua, named after a local langoustine-like crustacean, is a very good seafood restaurant in Campeche where he cooks. This seaport on the Gulf coast of the Yucatán was historically plagued by pirates, many of them English, and according to the Spanish one of them was named Francis Drake. The owner of La Pigua has named a few of his dishes after the pirates – Sir Francis squid, spaghetti Blackbeard and Lorencillo shrimp salad. Sir Francis squid also appears as Sir Francis octopus, which is what I had on the day, but I like to use our fresh local squid, which is wonderful with the flavours of guajillo chilli, garlic and lime juice. I'm sure Carlos won't mind that I have turned what was a main course into what's almost a tapas. He's that sort of a man, very skilful but understated.

SERVES FOUR AS A STARTER

2 tbsp olive oil
350g squid (prepared weight), cut into rings
¼ tsp salt
20 turns black peppermill
20g almonds, skin on, chopped
4 new potatoes (about 300g), freshly boiled and sliced thickly
1 dried guajillo chilli, seeds shaken out, sliced into rings
½ tsp sweet paprika
1 clove garlic, thinly sliced
125ml *Shellfish stock* (page 300)
Juice of ½ lime
A few sprigs of coriander

Heat the olive oil in a heavy frying pan over a high heat. Season the squid with salt and pepper and fry it for 2 minutes – if you have the tentacles, chuck them in too.

Add the almonds, sliced potatoes, chilli rings, paprika and garlic, fry for another minute, then pour in the shellfish stock. Stir, add the lime juice and cook until the sauce has reduced and coats the ingredients. Serve immediately, garnished with a little coriander.

OCTOPUS, PUERTA VALLARTA STYLE

This recipe comes from Diana Kennedy, described by *Saveur* magazine as 'the Julia Child of Mexico'. She said that was nonsense, but given her scholarly approach to recipes from all over the country, and her excellent cookery books, I think they have a point. She got this octopus dish from a restaurant in Puerto Vallarta, a city famed for its seafood cookery. I've changed the recipe slightly to simmer the octopus in water first, while she cooks it in the sauce from raw. I think that tends to make the sauce and octopus a bit too strong. She probably won't be pleased, but as she says herself, 'To me, the interesting part of cooking is bringing flavour out of ingredients, not having to put flavours in'.

**SERVES FOUR
AS A STARTER**

900g octopus, cleaned
 but not cut up
Salt
5 guajillo chillies
300g fresh tomatoes
4 cloves garlic, unpeeled
50ml olive oil
1 onion, chopped
12 peppercorns
1 tsp oregano
2 cloves
1½ tsp sugar

Put the octopus in a pan, add 600ml of water and a teaspoon of salt. Simmer the octopus for 35 minutes. Remove it from the pan, allow it to cool, then cut it into 2cm pieces. Reserve the cooking water.

Remove the seeds from the chillies and toast the chillies on both sides in a dry pan, along with the tomatoes and garlic. Remove the chillies first – you don't want to burn them, just intensify their flavour. Soak the chillies in 300ml of just-boiled water for 20 minutes to rehydrate them.

Continue to cook the tomatoes and garlic until the skins are brown. Peel the garlic cloves and slice them roughly, then quarter the tomatoes.

Heat the oil in a frying pan add the onion and garlic and cook over a medium heat for about 5 minutes. Pour the contents of the pan into a blender, then add the tomatoes and the soaked and drained chillies. Add the peppercorns, oregano, cloves, sugar and a teaspoon of salt and blend until smooth.

Tip the contents of the blender back into the frying pan and add half the octopus cooking water. Cook until the salsa is reduced by three-quarters, then stir in the cooked octopus and simmer for another couple of minutes.

Serve in little bowls as a first course, accompanied by corn tortillas or crusty bread.

MONKFISH, MUSSEL & PRAWN STEW WITH CHAR-GRILLED SOURDOUGH

The Tadich Grill is the oldest restaurant in California. It first opened in 1849 and you could almost say it hasn't changed much since then. When you walk in you are greeted by waiters in white jackets, black trousers and long white aprons, and the long wooden bar runs all the way down the centre of the restaurant. The kitchen, too, felt like it's been there forever and was as hot as my first little kitchen at The Seafood Restaurant used to be, mainly because, like me, they had a large mesquite charcoal grill. Mine was ordinary charcoal but the mesquite boiler at the Tadich is part of what makes it special. The queues at busy times are enormous and they serve on average 700 meals a day. This cioppino, which literally means chopped seafood, is famous and was delicious. There was an amazing variety of seafood but the important element was the chunky tomato base. They were generous enough to give me the recipe but I confess I had to cut out a few elements, mostly some seafood. The variety was simply too great for domestic shopping and purses.

SERVES FOUR TO SIX

12 raw shell-on prawns
700ml *Fish stock* (page 300)
  or water
3 tbsp red wine vinegar
1 tbsp sugar
30ml olive oil
30g butter
5 cloves garlic, chopped
½ medium onion, chopped
1 stick celery, chopped
1 green pepper, deseeded
  and chopped
100ml white wine
1 tsp salt
10 turns black peppermill
½–1 tsp chilli flakes
400g tin chopped tomatoes
1 tsp oregano
250g monkfish fillet,
  cut into 4cm pieces
20 raw mussels, cleaned

To serve
6 slices sourdough bread
1 clove garlic, peeled
Olive oil
Small handful parsley,
  chopped

Remove the heads and shells from the prawns but leave the last tail segment of the shell in place. Simmer the heads and shells in the stock or water for 20 minutes, then strain and discard them. Set the stock aside and reserve the prawn meat to add to the stew later.

Bring the vinegar and sugar to the boil in a small pan and reduce to a couple of teaspoons.

Heat the olive oil and butter in a saucepan, add the garlic, onion, celery and green pepper and sweat for 6–8 minutes. Add the white wine, salt, pepper, chilli flakes, tomatoes, then the fish stock and the vinegar reduction. Simmer for 30 minutes, adding the oregano for the last 5. You can make this base in advance if you like.

To finish, bring the stew base to the boil. Add the reserved raw prawns, the monkfish and mussels, put a lid on the pan and cook for 5 minutes. Toast the sourdough, then singe the slices slightly on a gas flame. Rub the toast with the garlic and sprinkle with olive oil.

To serve, place a slice of the toast in each bowl, ladle in some stew and sprinkle with parsley.

MEXICAN PRAWN COCKTAIL WITH TOMATO, AVOCADO & CHIPOTLE

It would be hard to wean any British person off prawn cocktail made with Marie Rose sauce (mayonnaise and tomato ketchup), but this is pretty special. Naturally it's quite spicy and smoky from the chipotle chilli but, as is so often the case in Mexico, the creamy element that I crave is supplied by ripe avocados. This dish comes from a rugged seafood restaurant called El Camello in the town of Tulum.

SERVES FOUR

375g medium prawns,
  cooked peeled and
  deveined
2 avocados, stoned,
  peeled and diced, then
  tossed in lime juice to
  prevent browning
2 tomatoes, chopped
Small handful of
  coriander, chopped
1 little gem lettuce, shredded
Lime wedges and *Totopos*
  (page 299), to serve

For the sauce
275ml tomato juice
4 tbsp extra virgin olive oil
Juice of 1 large lime
2 cloves garlic, peeled
½ red onion,
  roughly chopped
2 tsp chilli sauce (Cholula,
  Tabasco or Huichol)
1 tsp Worcestershire sauce
2 heaped tbsp *Chipotles en
  adobo* (page 298 or bought)
¼ tsp salt
8 turns of black peppermill

To make the sauce, put the tomato juice, oil, lime juice, garlic, onion, chilli sauce, Worcestershire sauce and chipotles en adobe in a blender or food processor. Season with salt and pepper, then blend until smooth. Refrigerate until ready to assemble the dish.

When you're ready to eat, mix the prawns with the sauce, diced avocado, tomatoes and three-quarters of the chopped coriander. Divide the shredded lettuce between 4 chilled cocktail or sundae glasses. Top with the prawn mixture, then sprinkle with the remaining coriander. Serve with lime wedges and the totopos on the side.

TOSTADAS DE ATÚN
RAW TUNA TOSTADAS

We ate in an excellent seafood restaurant in Mexico City called Contramar and there's a nice recipe from there for grilled bream on page 124. These tostadas were the first course that day, and as far as I recall the most popular dish. Subsequently I've eaten the same thing in the Yucatán, Baja California and Puerto Vallarta. They are impossibly easy to make and always loved. Serve with or without the chipotle crema.

**SERVES FOUR
TO EIGHT**

250ml corn oil
12–16 x 10cm *Corn tortillas*
    (page 44 or bought)
Guacamole (page 105)
450g sushi-grade tuna,
    cut into 1cm dice
2 ripe tomatoes, peeled,
    deseeded and diced
1 small banana shallot,
    chopped, or 2 spring
    onions, finely sliced
1–2 limes, cut into wedges
½ tsp salt
10 turns black peppermill
1 tbsp chopped coriander
Chipotle crema
    (page 298 – optional)

Heat 1–2 cm of corn oil in a frying pan to 180°C. Fry the tortillas for up to 30 seconds each side or until crisp and golden, then drain them on kitchen paper to remove excess oil. Alternatively, preheat the oven to 200°C/Fan 180°C, brush the tortillas on both sides with oil and bake them on a baking sheet for 3–5 minutes, until they are crisp and golden.

Spread the tortillas with guacamole and top with the tuna, diced tomatoes and shallot, then squeeze over some lime juice. Season with salt and pepper and top with chopped coriander. Serve with some chipotle crema on the side if you like.

SARDINES IN TORTILLAS WITH SPICY TOMATO SAUCE

Pan de cazon, literally translated as bread with dogfish, is a dish popular in Campeche on the Gulf of Mexico in Yucatán. I had it a few times and liked it but I was surprised to find that the dogfish tasted more like tinned sardines. One of the dilemmas writing books about a national cuisine is what to do about things we can't get here easily. Dogfish is not common in the UK these days, although it used to be, and it's generally considered to be a species that's endangered here. So I tried making this with a couple of tins of sardines and it was really lovely – a combination of the fish in a slightly spicy tomato sauce in a sandwich of crisp tortillas topped with avocados. I can't say too often how much I love the way the Mexicans combine something crisp with a sauce, so you get a satisfying textural complexity. The salad panzanella, with tomatoes and dry bread, works in the same way.

SERVES FOUR AS A STARTER

250g sardines in olive oil, drained
250ml corn oil, for frying
12 x 10cm *Corn tortillas* (page 44 or bought)
200g *Refried beans* (page 104), warmed
1 avocado, stoned, peeled and sliced

For the tomato sauce
2 tbsp olive oil
1 medium onion, sliced
1 clove garlic, chopped
1 tsp dried epazote (optional) or oregano
½ –1 habanero chilli, stem and seeds removed, roughly chopped
600ml passata (sieved tomatoes)
12 turns black peppermill
Salt, to taste

To make the sauce, heat the oil in a saucepan and sweat the onion, garlic, epazote or oregano and chilli until very soft. Add the passata and cook for 15–20 minutes. Liquidise the sauce in a blender or food processor and season with pepper and salt to taste.

Reserve one-third of the tomato sauce for finishing the dish, then put the rest back in the pan and add the sardines. Cook for about 15 minutes until the fish has broken up and combined with the tomato sauce – the sauce should be quite thick and most of the liquid evaporated.

Heat the corn oil in a frying pan and fry the tortillas for 1–2 minutes until crisp. Drain them on kitchen paper. Spread 8 of the tortillas with refried beans. Place one on each of 4 plates and spoon on some of the sardine 'stew'. Top with a second bean-covered tortilla, bean-side up, then add a bit more of the sardine stew. Finish with a third tortilla, then divide the reserved tomato sauce between the tortilla stacks and garnish with a few slices of avocado. Serve at once.

SEAFOOD DUMPLINGS WITH A SPICY DRESSING

Chinatown in San Francisco is the most famous Chinatown of any city in the world and it's still a residential community, whereas many others are just commercial centres. Martin Yan is the city's most famous Chinese chef and very engaging. He took me round every part, including a fortune cookie factory, which now makes fortune cookies for adults only. This inspired me to remember a suggestion from my wife Sas to alleviate the boredom of the inevitable homilies in every Chinese restaurant: add the words 'in bed'. For instance, 'you should be able to undertake anything – in bed'. I opened a few and added 'in bed' and it was hilarious, but I'm not sure that Martin saw the joke. Then we went to his wonderful restaurant in a Westfield shopping mall. It was a bit of a change from the hundred-year-old painted wooden houses and wooden streets, but the cooking was really inspired and these dumplings filled with scallops and prawns are a good example.

SERVES FOUR (24 DUMPLINGS)

For the dumpling dough
210g plain flour, sifted,
    plus extra for rolling
Large pinch of fine salt

For the filling
225g raw peeled prawns,
    finely chopped
225g scallops,
    finely chopped
¼ tsp salt
¼ tsp white peppercorns,
    crushed in a pestle
    and mortar

For the spicy dressing
2 spring onions, chopped
Small handful of
    coriander, chopped
20g root ginger,
    peeled and grated
2 cloves garlic,
    peeled and grated
2 tbsp vegetable oil
2 tbsp Sriracha chilli sauce
6 tbsp rice wine vinegar
4 tbsp soy sauce
4 tbsp toasted sesame oil
2 tbsp caster sugar

Mix the flour and salt with 100ml of water and knead for 5 minutes until smooth. You can do this by hand or, better still, in a food mixer with a dough hook. It will be a fairly tough dough. Leave the dough to rest for 20 minutes, covered with a tea towel, while you prepare the filling and dressing.

Mix the chopped prawns, scallops, salt and white peppercorns in a bowl, cover with cling film and refrigerate for at least 10 minutes. Mix all the dressing ingredients in a bowl, then cover and refrigerate.

When the dough has rested, divide it into 4 balls. Roll each ball into a sausage shape about 2.5cm thick, then divide this into 6. Roll each piece into a ball and with a rolling pin flatten it into a disc, 8–10cm in diameter. Use just enough flour on the surface to keep the dough from sticking.

Spoon a heaped teaspoon of filling into the centre of each disc. Fold it over into a semi-circle and, using your fingers, crimp the edges like a pasty.

Bring a large pan of water to the boil. Lower the dumplings into the water and boil for 6–8 minutes – they will rise to the surface when cooked. Drain well and serve with the spicy dressing.

HOG ISLAND OYSTERS WITH A CHILLI, CORIANDER & LIME DRESSING

The Hog Island Oyster Company sounds so Californian. The oyster-cleaning plant and restaurant is on the mainland near Petaluma, just north of San Francisco, and the oyster beds are around Hog Island, so named because early settlers kept pigs there; it was ideal, as they couldn't run away. I was much taken with the owner Terry Sawyer, partly because he turned out to have been to my restaurant in Padstow and also he'd visited virtually all the oyster suppliers I use in the UK. There is a network of oyster suppliers all over the world and everyone knows everyone. I would also add that if you're in the area of Petaluma and you have an open-topped Mustang to drive, it is the most glorious country to motor through on a sunny spring day with the stereo on loud.
I know. I was that oyster lover.

30 fresh oysters, shucked

For the dressing (enough for about 30 oysters)
60ml mirin
60ml rice vinegar
1 large shallot,
    very finely chopped
1 large jalapeño pepper,
    seeded, very finely
    chopped
Handful coriander,
    finely chopped
Juice of 1 lime
8 turns black peppermill

Mix the dressing ingredients in a bowl. When you're ready to eat, stir the sauce well to combine and serve it in a ramekin or small, shallow bowl to spoon over freshly shucked raw oysters.

A STEW OF TUNA WITH BLACK BEANS & ROASTED CHILLIES

Tommy Gomes runs a seafood warehouse in San Diego and like many Californians he's very concerned about conservation. Not only is all the fish and shellfish he sells from sustainable sources but he is also committed to persuading people to use every possible part of the fish, which is something I'm afraid we're not very good at in this country. He was very excited to show me an opah, an enormous round-bodied fish which swims along the surface of the sea, and was quite surprised that I knew all about them via my Australian connections. He made a fish version of chilli con carne using the belly flap of an opah. I've made this dish unashamedly using tinned tuna because by the time Tommy had finished the dish, the fish was slow cooked. Tommy used a couple of bought-in sauces, but I've made everything but the tuna from fresh and it's really good.

SERVES FOUR

2 guajillo chillies,
   seeds shaken out
2 pasilla chillies,
   seeds shaken out
6 tomatoes
2 tbsp corn oil
1 medium onion, chopped
2 cloves garlic, chopped
1 red pepper, diced
1 yellow pepper, diced
½ courgette, diced
½ tsp ground cumin
1 tsp dried oregano
2 tbsp *Chipotles en adobo*
   (page 298)
1 tsp salt
100g *Black beans* (page 102)
   or use 200g tinned
2 x 160g tins tuna steaks,
   drained

To serve
Small handful of coriander,
   roughly chopped
1 lime, cut into wedges
1 avocado, stoned,
   peeled and diced
1 green jalapeño chilli,
   finely sliced

Toast the dried chillies in a dry heavy frying pan for a couple of minutes until they are fragrant but not coloured. Remove them from the pan, put them in a bowl and cover with about 300ml of just-boiled water. Leave them to soften for about 20 minutes, then drain and reserve the soaking liquid. Dry roast the tomatoes in the pan until they have brown spots on the skin and have started to soften.

Heat the corn oil in a saucepan and gently fry the onion and garlic over a medium heat. When they're soft, add the diced peppers, courgette and the cumin and continue to cook for 5 minutes.

Meanwhile, put the drained chillies in a blender with 125ml of their soaking water, then add the oregano, tomatoes, skin and all, and whizz to a smooth sauce. Add the chilli and tomato sauce and the chipotles to the pan with the onions and peppers, then stir to combine until you have thickish sauce. Season with salt. Stir in the black beans and tuna and cook for a few minutes to heat everything through.

Serve sprinkled with coriander and with lime wedges, avocado and jalapeño slices on the side. Some boiled rice or tortillas are good accompaniments.

BAKED CRAB WITH POBLANO, ACHIOTE & CORIANDER

This dish comes from the restaurant of La Lomita, one of the best wineries in the Guadalupe Valley. The chef there is called Sheyla Alvarado. It was one of those occasions when I had no expectations of any great food until I tried this crab dish, scented with achiote and pasilla chilli. I should have asked for the recipe, but we had to leave for more filming so this is my interpretation. La Lomita is well worth a visit, as is their restaurant. If you feel robust, order their delicious 'Pagano' Grenache. I say robust because it is 15.8% alcohol. And if the owner Fernando Pérez Castro is there, have a chat with him. He's very good news!

SERVES SIX AS A STARTER

1 pasilla chilli, seeds shaken out
100g salted butter
1 large red onion, diced
3 cloves garlic, chopped
20g achiote paste, softened
2 tbsp orange juice
2 poblano chillies, deseeded and finely sliced, or 3–4 tbsp canned rajas
3 large tomatoes, deseeded and diced
250g white crab meat
Small handful fresh coriander, chopped
½ tsp salt
30g panko breadcrumbs
30g Parmesan cheese, grated
Totopos (page 299), to serve

Soak the pasilla chilli in just-boiled water for about 20 minutes, then drain and chop it.

Melt the butter in a pan and sweat the onion and garlic for 3–4 minutes until softened. Using the back of a spoon, mix the achiote paste to a paste with the orange juice in a small bowl, then add it to the onions together with the pasilla chilli, the poblanos, or rajas, and the tomatoes. Cook for 4–5 minutes before stirring in the crab meat to heat through. Stir in the chopped coriander, then taste and season with salt.

Divide the mixture between 6 ramekins. Mix the panko breadcrumbs with the cheese and sprinkle over the ramekins, then grill under a preheated grill for a few minutes until the tops are crisp and golden. Serve with totopos on the side for dipping.

FRIED PACIFIC SAND DABS WITH PARSLEY BUTTER

This was cooked for me by Bert Cutino at the Sardine Factory in Monterey, California. Ted Balestreri and Bert, who've had the restaurant for many years, are a highly entertaining pair of septuagenarians of Sicilian origin. They were very happy to point out that Clint Eastwood had sat 'just there' at their bar during the filming of *Play Misty For Me*. They took me into the kitchen and while Bert cooked, Ted entertained me with hilarious tales of the early days of the restaurant in the 70s, which reminded me of my own experiences. They both remarked that sand dabs are as good as our Dover soles. I did point out that the texture wasn't a patch on Dovers, but I think they had a point about the flavour. You could make this with fillets of Dover sole instead of our humble dab or plaice.

SERVES TWO

100g fine white breadcrumbs
25g Parmesan cheese, grated
1 clove garlic, grated
1 tsp finely chopped parsley
½ tsp finely chopped thyme
1 tsp finely chopped basil
4 sand dab fillets, each about
    75g (total 300g), or plaice
    or sole, skin on or off
40g plain flour, seasoned
    with black pepper
    and salt
1 egg, beaten
30g butter
1 banana shallot,
    finely chopped
1 clove garlic, finely chopped
300g new potatoes, boiled
    in their skins and halved
100g Swiss chard, tough
    stalks removed, washed
    and roughly torn
45ml olive oil

Maître d'hôtel butter
50g butter
1 tbsp finely chopped
    flatleaf parsley
1 tsp lemon juice
Pinch salt
6 turns black peppermill

Mix the ingredients for the maître d'hôtel butter in a small bowl and put it in the fridge until needed.

Mix the breadcrumbs with the Parmesan, garlic and herbs and spread on a plate. Dust the dab fillets with the seasoned flour, dip them into the beaten egg, then coat in the breadcrumb mixture. Set them aside.

Heat the butter in a pan over a medium heat and sweat the shallot and garlic until soft but not browned. Add the cooked potatoes and the chard and cook until the potatoes are warmed through and the chard has wilted.

In a separate non-stick frying pan, heat the olive oil over a medium to high heat and fry the coated dab fillets for about 2 minutes on each side until golden and crisp. Drain them on kitchen paper. Wipe out the pan, add the maitre d' butter and warm it through.

Divide the potato and chard mixture between 2 plates and serve with 2 dab fillets per person and pour over the hot butter sauce. Serve immediately.

POLLERIA
"CHALINO"
MAYOREO y MENUDEO

CHAL

POLLO FRE
DEL DIA
EN SUS DIFER
CORTES.

* PECHUGA
* PIERNA y M
* RETAZO
* MENUDEN
* CHORIZO
ALITAS
RNE M
CINA
NO DE

POLLERIA CHALINO

SERVICIO A DOMICILIO
QUEJAS y SUGERENCIAS A LOS TELS.
951=188 64 85
951=262 0321
PRECIO ESPECIAL A COCINAS
y BANQUETERIA

FACTURA ELECTRONICA

POULTRY

"POLLOS" ASADOS

Chicken tinga, along with carnitas, birria and barbacoa, is the foundation of a well-balanced taco. Tacos made from comforting meat or poultry, with the addition of fresh and assertive flavours like green chilli salsa, raw onion, sliced radishes, coriander and lime juice, are at the heart of Mexican cuisine. In the recipe on page 204 the chicken is first poached, then shredded and added to a sauce made with chipotles en adobo, tomatoes, oregano, garlic and onions. A batch made with a whole chicken can feed a crowd and this is a great advantage of Mexican food – a little poultry or meat in corn tortillas, with all the additions, goes a long way. It's food for people with not a lot of money but a love of good and inventive cooking. Chicken tinga also appears in a great recipe for tamales on page 80. Until I discovered this recipe in Puerto Vallarta, tamales – steamed corn dough wrapped in corn husks – had been the one Mexican dish I couldn't see the point of. I'd always found them bland but tamales with a centre of spicy chicken tinga changed my opinion. There is something really interesting about the taste of corn when contrasted with spicy and smoky flavours.

I was surprised to find relatively few recipes for turkey in Mexico, since they are native both there and in the United States. They used to do mole poblano with turkey but generally prefer chicken so I've come up with a recipe for turkey breast with chilli butter (page 218). I marinate the turkey in pasilla chilli, garlic, chipotle and cider vinegar, then roast the breast and make a gravy from the marinade.

Turning to California, I went to Martin Yan's restaurant called MY China, in San Francisco and watched the chefs create massive strings of egg noodles by hand. I came up with a chicken noodle soup dish to do justice to their superb noodles. Another dish I think is of special interest is the green chicken pozole with tomatillos, jalapeños and hominy grain on page 202. I think it's a particularly good recipe, not mine I hasten to add, and I felt it important to have at least one pozole, a dish that dates right back to Aztec times.

GREEN CHICKEN POZOLE

Pozole is undoubtedly pre-Hispanic and one of the oldest recipes in Mexico. There's something incredibly satisfying and comforting about savoury dishes made with corn, and the other secret of a great pozole is a good stock – in this case chicken. Nora Valencia, who made this for me, is an excellent cook. I'm conscious of a slight weakness in this book of not having spent enough time cooking in Mexican houses, so an afternoon with Nora was really welcome.

SERVES SIX

1 small chicken (about 1.3kg)
1 bouquet garni, made
   up of 6 cloves garlic,
   1 tbsp chopped thyme,
   ¼ tsp cumin seeds,
   4 cloves, 3 allspice berries
   and 1 small onion, halved,
   all wrapped in muslin
1½ tsp salt

For the green paste
100g green pumpkin seeds
1 tbsp lightly packed fresh
   oregano leaves
2 green jalapeño or
   serrano chillies
3 cloves, ground in pestle
   and mortar, or pinch
   of ground cloves
1 sprig of tarragon
A small handful of rocket
A few fronds of fennel leaves
6 cloves garlic, peeled
2 x 340g tins of tomatillos,
   drained
2 tbsp olive oil
850g tin of hominy
   (page 305)

To serve
5 radishes, finely sliced
2 green lettuce leaves,
   shredded
2 jalapeño chillies, sliced
1 small onion, finely chopped
2 limes, cut into wedges

Put the chicken in a large saucepan and cover it with water (you'll need about 2.5 litres). Add the bouquet garni and a teaspoon of the salt. Bring to the boil, then turn the heat down to a very gentle simmer and poach the chicken for 35–40 minutes.

Once the chicken is cooked, remove it and leave it to cool. Strain and reserve the stock. When the chicken is cool enough to handle, remove and discard the skin and bones. Using your fingers, shred the meat into bite-sized pieces and set it aside.

Toast the pumpkin seeds in a dry frying pan for a few minutes until they puff up and pop. Keep moving them so they don't burn. Put them into a food processor with the oregano, chillies, ground cloves, tarragon, rocket, fennel, garlic and tomatillos. Blend well, then add about 500ml of the reserved poaching stock to loosen.

Pour the mixture into a large pan, then rinse out the processor with the remaining stock and add it to the pan. Add the drained hominy and simmer for 10 minutes. Lastly, add the shredded chicken and remaining half teaspoon of salt to the pan and cook for a further 10 minutes, making sure the chicken is fully heated through.

Divide the hominy and chicken meat between warmed bowls and top up each bowl with green soup. At the table, garnish the pozole with radishes, lettuce, chillies and onion (the bandera colours of the Mexican flag). Serve with lime wedges.

TINGA DE POLLO

CHICKEN TINGA – PULLED CHICKEN WITH A SMOKY TOMATO SAUCE

This great dish, found all over Mexico, has a deep smoky flavour and is ideal for filling tacos, tostadas, burritos, tamales or empanadas. Make a batch using a whole chicken and you can feed a crowd or freeze half for later use.

SERVES FOUR TO SIX

1 whole chicken (about 1.3kg)
1 onion, peeled and halved
1 carrot, scrubbed and
    cut into 3
1 celery stick, cut in half
1 garlic clove, bashed
1 sprig of thyme or bay leaf

For the sauce

3–4 tbsp *Chipotles en adobo*
    (page 298), to taste
4 ripe tomatoes, quartered
1 tsp oregano
150ml chicken stock
    (from poaching the chicken)
1 tsp salt
2 tbsp olive or vegetable oil
2 medium onions, sliced
2 cloves garlic, chopped
10 turns black peppermill

To serve

As a filling for tacos
    or tostadas, serve
    with shredded lettuce,
    soured cream, crumbled
    Lancashire or feta cheese,
    chopped onion, chopped
    coriander, sliced radishes,
    lime wedges

Put the chicken in a large saucepan with the vegetables, garlic and thyme or bay leaf and add cold water to cover. Place the pan over a medium-high heat, bring the water to the boil, then skim off any foam that rises to the top. Turn the heat down, so the surface just blips from time to time, and poach the chicken for 30–40 minutes. Turn off the heat, remove the chicken from the pan and leave it until cool enough to handle. Strip off the meat and discard the skin and bones. Strain the stock and reserve 150ml for the sauce and keep or freeze the rest for soup or tamale dough.

For the sauce, put the chipotles en adobo, tomatoes and oregano in a blender with the 150ml of chicken stock and salt. Whizz to a smooth sauce, and then set aside.

Heat the oil in a saucepan and fry the sliced onions and garlic over a medium heat until soft and golden. Turn the heat up to high for a minute, and then tip in the tomato and chilli mixture. Cook for 5–10 minutes to reduce and thicken the sauce, then add the chicken meat. Taste for seasoning, add black pepper and a little more salt if required.

The tinga is now ready to use. It can be made in advance and reheated, but if using to fill tamales or empanadas, allow it to cool fully first.

CHICKEN WITH ORANGE, FENNEL & ZA'ATAR

I've mentioned a really happy lunch on a houseboat in Sausalito when a bunch of women turned up with some very Californian dishes (page 126). This chicken, made by our hosts Paula and Cory, was one I particularly liked. It's a combination of fennel, orange and ouzo plus za'atar, a Syrian blend of sesame seeds, sumac, cinnamon, coriander, fennel and oregano. To me, it's another example of how well Californian fusion food works.

Recipe photograph overleaf

SERVES FOUR TO SIX

Leaves from 2 sprigs
  of thyme
3 tbsp olive oil
3 tbsp ouzo (or other
  anise-based liqueur)
Juice of 1 lemon
½ tsp chilli flakes
1 tsp smoked sweet paprika
1½ tbsp za'atar
1 tsp fennel seeds, crushed
  in pestle and mortar
1 x 1.8kg chicken,
  jointed into 8 pieces,
  or 8 chicken thighs
2 navel oranges
1 large fennel bulb
  (about 375g), trimmed
  and cut into wedges
12 turns black peppermill
1 tsp flaked sea salt
Handful flatleaf parsley,
  roughly chopped.

Mix the thyme, olive oil, ouzo, lemon juice, chilli flakes, paprika, za'atar and fennel seeds in a large bowl. Add the chicken pieces and rub the mixture into them well.

Scrub the oranges, then slice each one into 4 rounds, leaving the skin on. Add the orange slices and fennel wedges to the bowl with the chicken, cover and refrigerate for 30 minutes to an hour.

Preheat the oven to 200°C/Fan 180°C. Put the chicken in a large ovenproof dish or roasting tin, keeping it in a single layer. Season with salt and pepper and bake for about 40 minutes. Scatter over the chopped parsley and serve.

LIME & CHICKEN SOUP

Portia Spooner, who helps me write my cookery books, had this lime soup when she was in Valladolid in Mexico doing research for the TV programme. She emailed me while she was at a restaurant near the famous Zaci Cenote to say how wonderful the soup was. Cenotes are the pools formed when porous limestone bedrock collapses and reveals the ground water underneath. They appear all over the surface of the Yucatán and are often connected by a system of subterranean waterways. Unfortunately, when I got there I was too busy jumping into the cenote to try the soup. I remember being filmed swimming in the enormously deep pool and remarking that there was something slightly unnerving about being in a small pool hundreds of metres deep, a sensation increased by the deep bluey-green colour to the water and by being nibbled at by blind fish.

SERVES SIX

3 chicken legs or
   4 chicken thighs
   (skin on and bone in)
2 onions, 1 roughly chopped,
   1 finely chopped
1 celery stick,
   roughly chopped
4 allspice berries
½ tsp black peppercorns
1½ tsp salt
2 tbsp corn or olive oil
3 cloves garlic,
   finely chopped
1 tsp dried oregano
½–1 habanero chilli,
   deseeded and
   finely chopped
2 large tomatoes,
   peeled, deseeded,
   cored and chopped
Juice of 3 limes

To serve
Fried tortilla strips
   (page 299)
2 avocados, stoned, peeled,
   and roughly chopped
Large handful coriander,
   roughly chopped
1–2 limes, sliced

Put the chicken pieces in a deep saucepan and cover them with cold water. Add the roughly chopped onion, the celery, allspice berries, peppercorns and salt. Bring to the boil, then turn down the heat and poach for 20–25 minutes. Remove the chicken with a slotted spoon and set it aside to cool. Strain and reserve the cooking liquid.

Heat the oil in a large saucepan and fry the finely chopped onion with the garlic, oregano and habanero until soft. Add the tomatoes, then the strained cooking liquid and the lime juice and cook gently for 20–25 minutes.

Remove the skin and bones from the chicken and shred the meat into bite-sized pieces. Add them to the soup and heat them through. Taste and season with salt. Ladle the soup into warm bowls. Divide the fried tortilla strips between the bowls and top with avocado, coriander and slices of lime.

MOLE POBLANO CON POLLO
CHICKEN MOLE POBLANO

I think it's important to stress that this book is not for purists. I have always had a problem with mole poblano, chilli and chocolate sauce, since I first tasted it in Mexico about 15 years ago and find it is often too sweet for our taste. Yet, I'm not unfamiliar with using chocolate in cooking, and a little in a rich red wine sauce works wonders. What I do like about mole poblano is the mixture of two dried chillies, mulato and pasilla, which gives the sauce a dark roasted fruitiness with just a hint of heat. The original recipe came from a convent in Puebla called the Dominican Convent of Santa Rosa and, by the way, if you are visiting the city it is definitely worth seeing the fabulous Talavera tiles. For gringos, I think my chicken mole is best served as a first course. *Recipe photograph overleaf*

SERVES EIGHT TO TEN AS A STARTER
4–5 skinless chicken breasts
2 tbsp corn oil
½ tsp salt
Toasted sesame seeds,
  to serve

For the mole
16 mulato or ancho chillies
  (about 200g)
4 pasilla chillies
30g stale baguette or white
  bread (about 1 slice)
50g sesame seeds
120g blanched almonds
1 tbsp coriander seeds
6 black peppercorns
5cm cinnamon stick
2 tbsp corn oil
1 small ripe plantain
  or an unripe banana,
  peeled and sliced
130g raisins or currants
1 onion, sliced
1 garlic clove,
  roughly chopped
Pinch of ground cloves
1 tsp oregano
1 litre *Chicken stock*
  (page 300)
100g dark chocolate
  (70–85% cocoa solids),
  chopped
1½ tsp salt

For the mole, rinse and clean the chillies. Remove the membranes, stems and seeds, reserving a few teaspoons of the seeds. Toast the chillies in hot dry frying pan for about 20 seconds until fragrant but not burnt, then soak them in a bowl of just-boiled water for 20 minutes. Drain and set aside.

Toast the bread, reserved chilli seeds, sesame seeds, almonds, coriander seeds, peppercorns and cinnamon stick until fragrant but not burnt. Set them aside to cool, then grind to a powder in a spice grinder.

Heat the corn oil in a separate pan and fry the plantain or banana. Add the raisins or currants and fry briefly, then add the onions and garlic and fry until the mixture is soft and sweet.

Put the fried contents of the pan, drained chillies, ground seeds and spices in a blender. Add the cloves, oregano and about 350ml of the chicken stock, then blitz to a smooth sauce. Wipe out the pan, then add the remaining stock and the chocolate to the pan along with the contents of the blender. Heat through gently for 15–20 minutes until the chocolate has melted and you have a thick dark 'gravy'. Do not allow it to boil. If the mixture is too thick, add a splash of water. Taste for seasoning and add a little salt if needed.

Coat the chicken breasts in corn oil and season them with salt, then brown them on both sides in a dry frying pan. Reduce the heat and continue to cook through for 10–15 minutes.

Slice the cooked chicken breasts on the diagonal and serve half a breast per person, with the sauce spooned over. Sprinkle with toasted sesame seeds.

PIPIAN ROJO

A RED STEW OF CHICKEN WITH ANCHO CHILLIES, PUMPKIN SEEDS & TOMATO

This poached chicken with ancho chillies, tomato and pumpkin seeds is very much Mexican home cooking. The recipe comes from a lady called Josefina Garcia, who opened a cenaduría (an evening food stall, normally outside the owner's house, selling home cooking) 60 years ago in Guadalajara. She's now in her 80s, has ten restaurants, called La Gorda, and this is still on the menu. It's basically chicken with a mole sauce made with the stock from poaching the chicken. We had a lovely morning with Josefina and her family. They still run all the restaurants and every day at about 11.30am they assemble at her house, children as well, and she cooks lunch for them. It's impossible to overstate the importance of the family in Mexican life.

SERVES FOUR TO SIX

1 whole chicken
  (about 1·6–1.8k)
1 onion, peeled and halved
1 carrot, scrubbed and
  cut into 3
1 celery stick, cut in half
1 garlic clove, bashed
1 bay leaf or sprig of thyme

For the pipián sauce
40g pumpkin seeds
2 ancho chillies, seeds
  shaken out and sliced
10g lard
3 cloves garlic,
  roughly chopped
½ onion, roughly chopped
1 red jalapeño, seeds in,
  roughly chopped
2 large ripe tomatoes,
  roughly chopped
50g maize flour
  (for tortillas or tamales)
About 700ml chicken
  poaching liquor
1 tsp salt

To serve
Mexican red rice (page 118)
Refried beans (page 104)

Put the whole chicken in a large pan with the vegetables, garlic and herbs and cover with cold water. Bring the water to the boil, skim off the scum, then turn down the heat and poach the chicken for 35–40 minutes. Turn off the heat and remove the chicken from the pan. When it's cool enough to handle, strip off the meat and put it in a flameproof casserole dish. Strain the poaching liquor and set it aside to use later in the sauce.

While the chicken is poaching, toast the pumpkin seeds and ancho chillies in a hot dry frying pan. Transfer them to a spice grinder and blend to a fine powder.

Heat the lard in a frying pan and fry the garlic, onion, jalapeño and tomatoes for 2–3 minutes. Add the ground pumpkin seeds and ancho chillies and the maize flour, then stir in the poaching liquor to make a gravy about the consistency of double cream. Season with salt. Transfer the contents of the pan to a blender and blitz to a smooth sauce. Tip it back into the pan, stir and simmer for 15 minutes adding more stock if needed.

Pour the sauce over the chicken in the casserole and heat through. Serve with Mexican red rice and refried beans.

CHICKEN NOODLE SOUP WITH YELLOW BEAN SAUCE

While at Martin Yan's restaurant in San Francisco I watched his very talented head chef create a massive string of thin egg noodles by hand. So I've come up with this chicken noodle dish which I hope does justice to the very best Chinese noodles. The soup, with its slices of poached chicken, pak choi, sugar snaps and bean sprouts is pleasant in its own right, but stir in the hot, sweet, sour and spicy sauce and you've got a super-charged soup.

SERVES SIX
1 whole chicken
    (about 1.5kg)
4 cloves garlic,
    peeled and sliced
30g fresh root ginger,
    finely sliced
1 star anise
1½ tsp salt
8 spring onions, sliced
    on the diagonal
300g dried egg noodles
2 small heads pak choi
100g sugar snap peas,
    cut on the diagonal
200g bean sprouts
1 tsp chilli flakes
2 tbsp toasted sesame oil
Bunch fresh coriander,
    roughly chopped

For the sauce
5 cloves garlic
25g fresh root ginger,
    peeled and chopped
1 red jalapeño chilli
2 tbsp brown sugar
2 tbsp rice wine vinegar
2 tbsp yellow bean sauce
2 tbsp dark soy sauce
1 tbsp white peppercorns,
    coarsely ground
½ tsp salt

Start by making the sauce. Put everything into a food processor and blend to a smooth paste.

Place the chicken in a large saucepan and cover it with 3.5 litres of water. Add the garlic, ginger, star anise, salt and 4 of the spring onions, then poach the chicken for 30 minutes. Strain the chicken from the stock and reserve the stock. Allow the chicken to cool, then slice the breasts and shred the meat from the rest of the bird and set it aside.

Put the strained stock into a clean pan and bring it to the boil. Turn down the heat to a simmer and add the noodles, pak choi, sugar snaps, bean sprouts, chilli flakes, sesame oil and the remaining spring onions. When the noodles and vegetables are cooked al dente, add the shredded chicken to heat through for a couple of minutes.

Serve the soup in bowls and add some sliced chicken breast. Sprinkle with chopped coriander and serve the spicy sauce alongside to stir into the soup.

TURKEY BREAST WITH PASILLA & CHIPOTLE CHILLI & BUTTER SAUCE

Although Mexico and the southern US are where turkeys come from there are precious few recipes for them in Mexican cuisine. It's traditional to serve mole poblano with turkey, but more often than not it's made with chicken. So I thought I would come up with my own roast turkey dish. I found that most supermarkets sell a butter-basted turkey breast joint, which serves three or four people, and I marinated this in the chilli salsa, then slow roasted it. I suggest serving it with Mexican red rice, or slicing it and rolling it up in tortillas with some pico de gallo salsa and avocado, but then it's also nice British style with roast potatoes and yes, some Brussels sprouts.

SERVES THREE TO FOUR

Butter-basted turkey
    breast joint (about 650g)
10g butter

For the marinade
1 pasilla chilli,
    seeds shaken out
3 cloves garlic
½ small onion, chopped
2 tsp cider vinegar
1 tsp salt
30g butter
1 heaped tsp *Chipotles en
    adobo* (page 298 or bought)
5g achiote paste
25g cashew nuts
1 tbsp dark brown sugar

Tear the pasilla chilli into 4 or 5 pieces and put them in a bowl with 200ml of just-boiled water. Leave to soak for 20 minutes. Put the chilli with its soaking water and the remaining marinade ingredients into a blender and blend until smooth. Pour one-third of this mixture over the turkey breast and rub it in all over. Cover and leave the turkey to marinate in the fridge for 1–2 hours.

Preheat the oven to 180°C/Fan 160°C. Put the turkey in a roasting tin and add 70ml of water. Roast for 45 minutes, then put the butter on top of the turkey and roast for another 5 minutes. Check the internal temperature of the turkey with a probe if you have one – it should be 70°C. Baste the turkey with the pan juices, then transfer it to a warm plate, cover with foil and leave it to rest for 5–10 minutes.

Add 100ml of water to the juices in the tin and deglaze over a medium heat. Add the remaining marinade and stir to combine. Simmer for 5–10 minutes, adding a little more water if the sauce looks too thick, then pass the sauce through a sieve.

Slice the turkey on the bias and serve with sauce spooned over and some Mexican red rice (page 118) or roast potatoes.

SAS'S CALIFORNIAN SOURDOUGH CHICKEN SANDWICH

This is really a celebration of great Californian sourdough bread. I've been ear bashing Paul Tippett, our baker back in Padstow, to produce a Californian sourdough, and I have to say we're getting close. The latest is really quite sour with plenty of air bubbles and is substantial in weight with a dark cracking crust. I asked my wife Sas what her perfect sourdough sandwich would be, given that she loves them and they do great sandwiches in Sydney like they do in California. This is her combination idea, or combo as she'd call it.

SERVES FOUR

4 large slices good-quality sourdough bread
1 tbsp extra virgin olive oil
1 small little gem lettuce, leaves sliced
2 skinless chicken breasts, poached for 10–12 minutes, then cooled
2 tomatoes, preferably a sweet, deep-flavoured heirloom variety, sliced
1 avocado, stoned, peeled and sliced
Salt and black pepper, to taste

For the dressing
1½ tbsp soured cream
1½ tbsp mayonnaise
1 heaped tsp *Chipotles en adobo* (page 298 or bought)

Mix the ingredients for the dressing together. Brush the slices of sourdough with the olive oil and toast them, then slightly singe them in a gas flame or on a hot electric element. Top the toast with sliced lettuce leaves.

Slice the chicken breast at an angle and lay the slices on top of the lettuce, followed by some tomato and avocado. Season with salt and black pepper, then drizzle over the dressing. Serve immediately.

MEAT

The Mercado Central in Cholula is, I suspect, not everyone's cup of tea, dedicated as it is to every part of the cow, the pig and the sheep, not to mention the goat. As you walk down the aisles, trotters, heads and entrails are hanging everywhere and there are great cauldrons of boiling fat for cooking sheets of pig skin until crisp to produce the Mexican version of pork scratchings, chicharrón. I remember thinking with some wistfulness that it's a shame markets like this don't exist back home any more. I think that once you've accepted meat eating, it's almost more respectful not only to eat every possible part of an animal but also to be aware of the reality.

As well as the meat counters, there were some really exciting food stalls, many specialising in lamb or beef barbacoa. This is yet another method of slow cooking meat and I particularly like the beef version flavoured with garlic, onions, cloves, lime juice and cider vinegar (page 234). Traditionally this dish was cooked in a pit in the ground but these days a slow oven is more practical. I've tried in the book to include every way of slow cooking meat, but I must confess I've missed out mixiote. This is because it is absolutely essential when slow cooking lamb in this way to wrap it in a paper-like membrane taken from the agave plant, famous for producing tequila and mescal. The flavour from the agave is supposed to be special, but it's rare to get mixiote cooked in anything but greaseproof paper, which isn't quite the point.

Interestingly, Mexicans don't tend to cook meat rare or medium rare over charcoal. Indeed, at a ranch just outside Oaxaca I watched with consternation as some local women grilled steak straight on the hot charcoal – it was like black leather when we came to eat it. It was a great relief to have chef Miguel Angel Guerrero cook me rare venison on the charcoal grill at his farm just outside Tijuana. I haven't written a recipe for underdone steak or lamb but I would recommend the same accompaniments that he did for his recipe on page 253.

Lastly, steak and eggs may not be the most astounding recipe in the book but it's a fond memory for me of finally getting a breakfast of steak and eggs in California. As a lover of Westerns, in which everyone seems to have steak for breakfast, that meal at Rudfords Diner in San Diego (page 235) was a high point of my trip.

ALBONDIGAS EN SALSA VERDE

MEATBALLS IN TOMATILLO & SERRANO SALSA

These are particularly well-flavoured meatballs. It's unusual to find hard-boiled egg right in the centre of a meatball, but it's rather a pleasing contrast. I had some difficulty deciding whether to use a green sauce or red sauce for this dish, as I've had plenty of both, but I think the slightly higher acidity of the salsa verde with tomatillos wins the day.

SERVES FOUR

300g minced beef
300g minced pork
75g white long-grain
   rice, uncooked
1 tsp dried oregano
1 tsp salt
½ tsp cumin
Pinch ground allspice
6 turns black peppermill
1 clove garlic, finely chopped
½ small onion, peeled and
   very finely chopped
1 egg, beaten
1 hard-boiled egg, diced
2 tbsp olive oil
Small handful chopped
   coriander, to garnish

For the sauce
1 large (794g) tin
   tomatillos, drained
1 green serrano or
   jalapeño chilli, stem
   removed, halved
½ onion, chopped
1 garlic clove, chopped
3 tbsp corn oil
½ tsp salt, to taste

To serve
Mexican red rice
   (page 118) or plain rice

Begin by making the meatballs. Put all the ingredients, except the hard-boiled egg, olive oil and coriander, in a bowl and mix well with your hands, then mould the mixture into 20 golfball-sized balls. Make an indent in each one with your finger, press in a piece of hard-boiled egg, then mould the meat mixture around it.

For the sauce, put the tomatillos, chilli, onion and garlic in a blender or food processor. Add 100ml of water and blend until smooth. Heat the oil in a large pan over a medium to high heat, then pour in the blended tomatillo mixture. Add salt to taste and simmer for 10–15 minutes.

Heat the olive oil in a frying pan and fry the meatballs, turning them gently until golden all over. Add them to the tomatillo sauce, cover with a lid and simmer for 25–30 minutes. Add water if the sauce starts to look too thick.

Garnish with chopped coriander and serve with Mexican red rice or plain boiled white rice.

CARNERO ASADO CON XNI-PEK
BBQ LAMB WITH SHREDDED CABBAGE

In the deepest Yucatán countryside, close to the town of Tizimin, I met Sam Critchley, a very well spoken, home counties Englishman who had fallen in love with a delightful Mexican girl called Alina while he was doing a year learning Spanish for a modern languages degree at Cambridge. His fellow undergraduates had elected to go to parts of Spain, but in a pioneering spirit Sam decided to explore Mexico. The result was that he married into Alina's family and has learnt the art of being a ranchero from his father-in-law. I was intrigued. The ranch was not a Dallas-style hacienda but a very rugged little property. At the ranch, three local ladies were sitting with a cross and candles on the table in front of them, saying prayers and singing in praise of San José, the patron saint of the ranch. It happened to be the day they hold an annual prayer ceremony and feast in his honour. This lamb dish with the superb coleslaw was the celebratory lunch. Sam loves the life of a Yucatán farmer and adores his new family. I soon saw why. As is so often the case in Mexico, the family was so welcoming.

SERVES FOUR

For the lamb
2 tbsp salt
2 cloves garlic, unpeeled
    and smashed
1 tbsp coarsely ground
    black pepper
100ml Seville orange juice
    or ordinary orange juice
1kg lamb chops

For the cabbage slaw
1 large onion, whole
    and unpeeled
250g green cabbage
150ml Seville orange juice
    or ordinary orange juice
250g ripe tomatoes, diced
Handful of coriander,
    chopped
1 tsp salt
10 turns of black peppermill
½ habanero chilli, finely
    chopped (optional)

To serve
Corn tortillas
    (page 44 or bought)

Light the barbecue. Mix the salt with 1.5–2 litres of water to make a brine and add the garlic, pepper and juice. Add the lamb chops and leave them to marinate for at least 30 minutes and up to 2 hours.

For the slaw, put the whole, unpeeled onion over charcoal to roast until well blackened and no longer crunchy in the middle. Remove it and leave it to cool down, then peel or rinse off the burnt outer layer. This takes a good 20–30 minutes and should be done while the meat marinates. The roasting is very important because it's where the sweetness comes from to offset the sourness – I often put the onion directly on to the hot coals to speed things up.

Meanwhile, roughly shred the cabbage with a sharp knife and mix it with the rest of the ingredients for the slaw in a bowl. When the onion is ready and peeled, chop it and add it to the slaw. Let it stand for at least 10 minutes.

Once the meat has marinated for at least 30 minutes, barbecue it until it's nicely charred around the edges and still a bit pink in the middle. Serve with the slaw and warmed corn tortillas (page 306).

BEEF BARBACOA WITH CHIPOTLE, GARLIC & OREGANO

Barbacoa is not the cooking of meat on grill bars over a charcoal or wood fire, though our word 'barbecue' comes from it. It's the slow cooking of beef, lamb, goat or pork, traditionally in a pit in the ground. Barbecuing in the southern part of the US is much closer to barbacoa than our cooking of sausages and chops in the back garden. I regard all the slow-cooked meats of Mexico, like carnitas (page 86) and pork pibil (page 94), as among the highlights of their cuisine. Coupled with salsas, guacamole, some chopped onion, tomato and coriander and plenty of warm tortillas, recipes like this allow you to feed lots of people effortlessly.

SERVES TEN TO TWELVE (OR MORE)

3 tbsp *Chipotles en adobo* (page 298 or bought)
1 onion, sliced
6 cloves garlic, chopped
5 cloves, ground
1 tsp oregano
100ml cider vinegar
Juice of 3 limes
2–2.5kg beef brisket joint
30g lard
2 tsp salt
500ml beef stock

To serve
Handful thinly sliced radishes
Pickled jalapeños, sliced
Handful coriander, roughly chopped
24–36 *Corn tortillas* (page 44 or bought), warmed (page 306)
Roasted red tomato and chilli salsa (page 108)
2–3 avocados, stoned, peeled and sliced
2–3 limes, cut into wedges

Mix the chipotles en adobo with the onion slices, garlic, cloves, oregano, cider vinegar and lime juice. Smear the mixture all over the beef, put the beef in a dish and cover well, then refrigerate for a couple of hours.

Drain the marinade from the beef and reserve it. Preheat the oven to 160°C/Fan 140°. Heat the lard in a large flameproof casserole dish (ideally one with a lid) and brown the brisket on all sides. Deglaze the pan with 150ml of water.

Add the reserved marinade to the pan together with the salt, beef stock and the brisket. Bring the liquid to the boil, then immediately cover the casserole with a tight-fitting lid or a double layer of foil and transfer it to the oven. Cook for about 4 hours, checking every hour or so and adding a little water if it looks like it is drying out.

When the meat is ready it should be very tender and easy to pull apart with two forks. Transfer it to a board while you reduce the cooking juices, if necessary, to about 250–300ml.

Once you have shredded the meat, mix it with the cooking juices to coat – the meat should be moist, not swimming in sauce. Serve it on a warm dish, topped with radishes, jalapeños and chopped coriander. On the side, serve warmed tortillas, roasted tomato salsa, sliced avocado and lime wedges.

GRILLED SIRLOIN STEAK WITH O'BRIEN POTATOES & EGGS

This recipe came about in San Diego because I insisted on our local fixer, that's the person who sorts out the permits, hotels and so on, taking us to a proper diner. I wanted somewhere with banquette seating, lots of vinyl and chrome, an ever-present jug of coffee, and waffles for breakfast. And, as it turned out, steak. I'd seen so many Westerns where the cowboys have steak and eggs for breakfast and it's what I wanted to do. It was divine. With every step of the ordering I was faced with serious choices: how would you like your eggs – sunny side up or over easy? White, brown or sourdough bread? How would you like your steak cooked? Would you like hash browns, house potatoes or O'Brien? I chose O'Brien's because they seemed to be a local delicacy. They were fried potatoes, but with onion and peppers and very nice they were too.

SERVES FOUR

4 x 140g sirloin steaks,
   at room temperature
20g butter, melted
Vegetable oil
4–8 eggs
salt and pepper

For the O'Brien potatoes
750g floury potatoes, peeled
30g butter
1 tbsp olive oil
1 medium onion, chopped
1 green pepper, deseeded
   and chopped
1 tsp salt
12 turns black peppermill
¼ tsp chilli flakes

Dice the potatoes into 2.5cm cubes and cook them in salted water until just tender, then drain them.

Heat the butter and oil in a large frying pan over a low heat and fry the onion and green pepper for 7–10 minutes until soft. Add the cooked potatoes, turn the heat up to medium and stir. The potatoes will break up a bit, then take on a crust on the corners and start to brown slightly. Season them with salt, black pepper and chilli flakes and keep them warm.

Heat a separate pan or griddle over a high heat until very hot. Brush the steaks with melted butter and season them with salt and pepper. Cook them to your liking (see below), then set them aside to rest, covered with foil, while you fry the eggs.

Heat some oil in a frying pan over a low to medium heat and fry the eggs, one or two per person. Serve with the steaks and the O'Brien potatoes.

Approximate timings for a 2cm-thick sirloin steak:
Blue: 1 minute each side
Rare: 1½ minutes each side
Medium rare: 2 minutes each side
Medium: 2¼ minutes each side
Medium to well done: 2½–3 minutes each side

CARNE CON CHILE

The classic chilli con carne made with beans and minced beef is more of a Tex-Mex recipe.
In Mexico home cooks make carne con chile for their families, using cubed beef or pork
in a rich chilli sauce with or without tomatoes, and with beans and or rice on the side.
Serve this with any number of your favourite toppings, such as shredded lettuce, soured
cream, crumbled Lancashire cheese, avocado, coriander, chopped onions and radishes.

**SERVES FOUR
TO SIX**

50g dried guajillo chillies,
  seeds shaken out
4 large ripe tomatoes, whole
4 cloves garlic, skin on
30g lard or 3 tbsp corn oil
1kg braising steak, cubed
1 large onion, chopped
1 tsp ground cumin
1 tsp dried oregano
4 allspice berries, bruised
1 bay leaf
1 tsp salt
2 tbsp *Chipotles en adobo*
  (page 298 or bought)
12–18 freshly made
  Corn tortillas
  (page 44 or bought)

For the toppings
Chopped coriander
Soured cream
Lancashire or feta
  cheese, crumbled
Avocado, stoned,
  peeled and diced
Onions, chopped
Radishes, sliced

To serve
Black beans (page 102)
  or *Mexican red rice*
  (page 118)

In a dry heavy-based frying pan, toast the guajillo chillies
until fragrant but not burnt. Transfer them to a bowl and
pour over 450ml of just-boiled water. Leave them to soak for
15–20 minutes. In the same pan, dry fry the tomatoes and
garlic until softened and charred. Set aside the tomatoes and
garlic until cool enough to handle, then peel off and discard
the garlic skins and quarter the tomatoes, skin and all.

Heat a tablespoon of lard or oil in a large flameproof
casserole and brown the cubes of beef all over. It's best to
do this in batches, adding another tablespoon of lard or oil
as needed. Transfer each batch of meat to a plate. Then add
the remaining lard or oil to the pan and fry the onion for
3–4 minutes until softened. Add the cumin, oregano, allspice
and bay leaf. Cook for 2 minutes, then turn off the heat.
Preheat the oven to 180°C/ Fan 160°C.

Put the soaked chillies and about 150ml of their soaking
liquid in a blender and add the garlic, tomatoes, salt and
chipotles en adobo. Blend until as smooth as possible, then
tip into the casserole with the onions and add the browned
beef. Stir in about 300ml of the chilli soaking water.
Reserve the rest in case you need more later.

Bring to the boil, then turn down to a simmer, cover
and cook for 1½ to 2 hours until the beef is tender. Check
the water a couple of times during cooking and make sure
that the meat doesn't dry out. Add a little more water if
necessary. While the meat is cooking, prepare the tortillas
and a selection of toppings. Serve with warmed tortillas
(page 306), toppings and beans or rice, if desired.

CHARLIE CHAPLIN'S GRILLED LAMB'S KIDNEYS WITH BACON

The Musso & Frank Grill opened on Hollywood Boulevard in 1919 and has been serving writers, producers, directors and stars ever since. When you first walk in it feels far too dark and plush, but then you realise it's a welcome hideaway from the fierce California sun. So many famous writers-turned-screenwriters, including Raymond Chandler, F. Scott Fitzgerald, William Faulkner and Dashiell Hammett, made it their base in Hollywood, perhaps escaping there for the famous martini after yet another script was savaged by a studio. Stars, too, such as Marilyn Monroe, Humphrey Bogart, Greta Garbo, and lately Johnny Depp and Brad Pitt, have all eaten here. The diner next to me at the bar told me I was in Steve McQueen's chair. This dish, Charlie Chaplin's favourite, is still on the menu. I liked the combination of the parsley lemon vinaigrette, with oregano, garlic and chopped anchovies, and the slightly pink kidneys with crisp bacon. A glass of Napa Chardonnay seemed to go very well with it.

SERVES FOUR

12 lamb's kidneys
8 rashers smoked
   streaky bacon
Salt
Black pepper

*For the parsley
   lemon vinaigrette*
1 tbsp chopped mint leaves
2 tbsp chopped flatleaf
   parsley
2 cloves garlic, chopped
1 shallot, chopped
15ml lemon juice
60ml olive oil
1 tsp lemon zest
1 tsp chopped oregano
½ tsp salt
1 anchovy, chopped

Whisk the ingredients for the vinaigrette together and set it aside while you prepare the kidneys.

Remove the outer membrane from the kidneys. Cut each kidney in half and trim away the white, fatty core. Take 4 metal skewers and slide 6 pieces of kidney on to each. Heat a grill or griddle pan to medium-high and grill the bacon rashers until crisp, then keep them warm.

Season the kidneys with salt and pepper and grill them for about 2 minutes. Turn them and cook for another 1–2 minutes or until the kidneys are cooked on the outside and pink in the middle. The timing here will vary depending on the strength of your grill and how pink you like your kidneys. Cook them for 3–4 minutes for more well-done meat.

Slide the kidneys off the skewers on to warmed plates and serve with the crispy bacon, vinaigrette and a green salad.

STUFFED CHILLIES WITH A WALNUT & POMEGRANATE DRESSING

I was convinced that this dish was Spanish, as it has so many Spanish /Moorish flavours, including sherry, pomegranates, walnuts and almonds, but it is from Puebla, and is said to have been created to celebrate Mexican independence from Spain. It is intended to show the colours of the Mexican flag, with the green poblano chilli, the white walnut and milk sauce, and the red pomegranate seeds. As luck would have it, we couldn't get poblano chillies when we cooked the dish for the photo so we had to use red romanos instead – but the coriander served us for the Mexican flag. I ate this at Casa Kimberly, Puerta Vallarta, a recently opened hotel which combines the houses of Richard Burton and Elizabeth Taylor on either side of the street. The houses were linked by a bridge to which I imagined Richard retreated after a particularly blistering 'who's afraid of Virginia Woolf' type row with Elizabeth. *Recipe photograph overleaf*

SERVES EIGHT

8 green poblano peppers
2 tbsp olive oil
100g celery, finely chopped
1 small onion, finely chopped
100g carrot, finely chopped
200g minced beef
200g minced pork
2 tbsp sweet sherry
30g raisins
25g candied mixed peel
50g flaked almonds
75g pecan nuts, chopped
Pinch of fresh thyme leaves
½ tsp dried oregano
½ tsp ground cinnamon
½ tsp salt
10 turns black peppermill

For the nogada sauce
300ml whole milk
50g pecan nuts
50g walnut pieces
75g cream cheese
50g ricotta or curd cheese
1 tbsp sweet sherry

To serve
Seeds of ½ pomegranate
8 sprigs of fresh coriander

Using a pair of tongs, char the peppers over a flame until blackened, then peel off the charred skin and set them aside.

For the filling, heat the olive oil in a frying pan over a low to medium heat and sweat the celery, onion and carrot for about 10 minutes until softened. Turn up the heat, add the beef and pork and fry until lightly browned, then add the sherry, raisins, candied peel, nuts, herbs and cinnamon and season with salt and pepper. Cook briefly, then remove from the heat and allow to cool to room temperature.

For the nogada sauce, blitz all the ingredients in a blender to a rich creamy consistency.

Very carefully slit down one side of each of the peppers and scrape out the seeds with a teaspoon. Fill the peppers with the meat and fruit mixture, then put them on a serving plate and drizzle over some of the sauce. Sprinkle with pomegranate seeds and coriander and serve with a bowl of the cold sauce so everyone can help themselves.

BIRRIA
LAMB, PASILLA & TOMATO STEW

A slow-cooked birria, spiced with oregano, cumin and allspice and served with lime, coriander and tortillas, is one of the great flavours of Mexico. You can add a hot salsa, but those four elements are perfection. The dish comes from the state of Jalisco and I have enthused about it from Guadalajara to Puerta Vallarta, where there is a little taquería called Tacos Robles on Calle Constitución that serves exceptional breakfast birria tacos. If you are not used to a slow-cooked lamb stew for breakfast, don't even think about going to Mexico.

SERVES FOUR

1 guajillo chilli, stem removed, seeds shaken out
1 pasilla chilli, stem removed, seeds shaken out
5 ripe tomatoes, quartered, hard cores removed
5 cloves garlic, unpeeled
½ medium onion, peeled
60ml cider vinegar
2 tsp dried oregano
½ tsp cumin seeds, ground
4 allspice berries, ground
1.5kg lamb, mutton or goat shoulder, on the bone, cut into 4–5 chunks (ask your butcher)
1½ tsp salt
10 turns black peppermill
3 tbsp lard or corn oil
½ medium onion, chopped
200ml lamb, beef or *Chicken stock* (page 300)

To serve
Large handful coriander, roughly chopped
12–16 *Corn tortillas* (page 44 or bought)
2 limes, cut into quarters

Heat a dry, heavy-based frying pan over a medium heat. Toast the chillies for a minute or so on each side until fragrant but not coloured, then put them in a bowl with 300ml of just-boiled water. Leave them to soak for about 20 minutes to soften.

Char the tomatoes, garlic and onion half in the pan until they are covered in black spots, then set them aside until cool enough to handle. Peel the tomatoes and garlic and put them in a blender with the charred onion half, the drained soaked chillies, cider vinegar, oregano, ground cumin and ground allspice berries. Blend to make a smooth sauce.

Season the meat with salt and pepper. Heat the lard or oil in a large flameproof casserole dish over a high heat and brown the meat in batches, turning it to brown on all sides. Add the chopped onion and brown it for a few minutes, then add the blended sauce and simmer for 5–10 minutes. Add the stock, cover the casserole with a lid and bring the contents to the boil. Immediately turn down the heat and leave to simmer very gently for 2–2¼ hours.

When the meat is tender and falling off the bone, remove it with a slotted spoon. Shred the meat with two forks and discard the bones. If there is a lot of sauce remaining in the pan, boil it hard to reduce so there is enough to loosely coat the shredded meat. Put the meat back in the pan and stir to combine. Scatter over the chopped coriander and serve with warmed tortillas (page 306) and lime quarters.

SLOW-COOKED SPICED LAMB WITH TORTILLAS & LIME

If you're travelling down Baja California, the Valle de Guadalupe is something of a must. Baja is Mexico's biggest wine growing state and Guadalupe Valley is held to be the best part. I'd heard so much about it that I expected a sort of Napa Valley, all green and gracious, but this is Mexico. It's dry and scruffy, with half-finished buildings everywhere and wineries with bits tacked on the side, but the wine is really good and I think it attracts wine-makers with a pioneering spirit. Like everywhere else in the valley, La Cocina de Doña Esthela isn't a romantic hacienda. It's a very basic building, surrounded by a farm which rears the animals they cook in the restaurant. The food is excellent and after a breakfast of say, lamb borrego – pulled barbacoa-style lamb – or perhaps a machaca (sun-dried beef) burrito and strong black coffee you will realise, along with the large crowds that come every day, that Doña Esthela is quite special. She's a completely committed cook, with awe-inspiring attention to detail, and because of her passion you can't help but be infected by her enthusiasm and joy. As the Mexicans say, she has *sazón* – she cooks well.

SERVES SIX TO EIGHT

2 pasilla chillies, stems removed, seeds shaken out
2 ancho chillies, stems removed, seeds shaken out
3 cloves garlic, unpeeled
1 tsp salt
1 tsp dried oregano
1.5–1.7kg lamb shoulder

To serve
24–32 x 15cm *Corn tortillas* (page 44 or bought)
1 onion, chopped
Handful coriander, roughly chopped
2 limes, cut into wedges

Toast the chillies and garlic cloves in a hot dry frying pan until fragrant. Transfer the chillies to a bowl, cover them with just-boiled water and leave them to soften for 20 minutes. Peel the garlic and put it in a blender with the salt, oregano and the soaked, drained chillies, then blitz with enough of the soaking water to make a fairly thick paste.

Pierce the lamb all over with a fork, rub it with the chilli paste and leave it to marinate for 2–4 hours. Preheat the oven to 170°C/Fan 150°C. Pour 150–200ml of water into the bottom of a large cast-iron casserole dish or a heavy roasting tin and add the lamb. Cover it with a lid or a couple of layers of tight-fitting foil and cook for 3–3½ hours or until the meat is very tender and falling off the bone.

Preheat your grill. Drain off the juices from the meat, place it on a baking tray and put it under the grill for 5–10 minutes until it's well browned on top. Shred the meat with two forks, then serve it with the cooking juices, warmed tortillas (page 306), chopped onion, coriander and some lime wedges.

FRIJOL CON PUERCO
PORK WITH BLACK BEANS

This very hearty pork stew comes from Yucatán, where traditionally it was served as a family meal on Mondays. It's usually accompanied by rice. The salsa to go with it is made with habanero chilli and and is naturally very hot. If you are not sure about it, remove the seeds from the chilli or use jalapeños instead. *Recipe photograph overleaf*

**SERVES FOUR
TO SIX**
25g lard
1kg pork shoulder,
    cut into 5cm chunks
1 onion, chopped
3 cloves garlic, chopped
450g pinto or Mexican
    black beans, rinsed
2 tsp dried epazote
    (optional) or oregano
1 tsp salt
10 turns black peppermill

For the chiltomate
600g ripe tomatoes
1 red habanero chilli,
    stem and seeds removed
½ small onion, chopped
1 clove garlic, peeled
1 tsp salt
2 tbsp corn oil

To serve
1 avocado, stoned,
    peeled and diced
2 limes, cut into wedges
Handful coriander,
    roughly chopped
6 radishes, finely sliced
18 *Corn tortillas*
    (page 44 or bought) or rice

Heat the lard in a large flameproof casserole dish over a high heat and brown the chunks of pork all over. Reduce the heat to medium, add the chopped onion and garlic and stir for a few minutes until softened. Add the black beans, epazote or oregano, salt, black pepper and 2–2.5 litres of water, then bring to the boil. Reduce heat to simmer and cook for 1¼–1½ hours.

While the beans and pork are cooking, make the sauce. Roast the tomatoes and the chilli in a dry, heavy-based frying pan until they are softened and covered with brown spots. Tip them into a blender, add the onion, garlic and salt and blitz to a smooth sauce. Heat the corn oil in a pan and when it's hot, add the contents of the blender. Simmer for 10–15 minutes, then pour the sauce into a jug or bowl. You can make it in advance and reheat when needed.

Serve the pork and bean stew topped with some of the chilli sauce and with the side dishes.

MAC 'N' CHEESE – MACARONI CHEESE WITH SMOKY BACON

In San Francisco I stayed at The Andrews Hotel in Post Street. Atmospherically it was perfection, a tall narrow building with quite small rooms and only one lift. A buffet breakfast was laid out on each floor, but for most meals I tended to go to the diner just down the road, a great bar across the street called The Owl Tree, or to an Italian restaurant nearby, which had such dishes as pasta and clams, carbonara and a mac 'n' cheese. To begin with I was a bit put off, as all the dishes seemed to have too much of everything – too much sauce, too much cream, too much cheese; not a bit like Italy. But then, while into my second glass of Sonoma Cutrer Russian River Chardonnay, I began to think to myself this isn't Italy, it's California, and if they want to re-interpret classic dishes why shouldn't they? Someone I met in Palermo once told me that the secret of good Italian dishes, as taught to her by her grandmother, is *esagerare* – put more of everything in – and so it is with this mac 'n' cheese recipe. There's masses of cheese and plenty of smoked bacon.

SERVES SIX TO EIGHT

100g butter, plus
  extra for greasing
100g plain flour
1 heaped tsp Dijon mustard
1.2 litres whole milk
5 tbsp double cream
1 bay leaf
400g mature Cheddar,
  grated
20 turns black peppermill
8 rasps freshly
  grated nutmeg
500g dried macaroni
100g smoked bacon lardons
  or smoked pancetta cubes
60g white breadcrumbs
50g Parmesan cheese,
  grated
Salt

Melt the butter in a large saucepan, stir in the plain flour and cook for a minute. Add the mustard, then take the pan off the heat and gradually whisk in the milk and cream. Add the bay leaf, put the pan back on the heat and cook the sauce, stirring constantly, until it boils and is thick and bubbling. Take the pan off the heat again, remove the bay leaf and add the Cheddar, then keep stirring until the cheese has melted. Season with black pepper and nutmeg.

Boil the macaroni in a large pan of salted boiling water (with a ratio of 1 teaspoon of salt per 600ml of water) for about 10 minutes or until al dente, then drain well.

Butter an ovenproof dish that's about 35 x 20cm in size and preheat the oven to 200°C/Fan 180°C. Fry the bacon lardons or pancetta until crisp and add them to the cheese sauce. Stir the cooked macaroni into the sauce and pour everything into the buttered dish. Mix the breadcrumbs with the Parmesan and scatter them over the top. Bake for 25–30 minutes until golden and bubbling. Serve with a green salad.

MENUDO
TRIPE SOUP WITH GUAJILLO CHILLIES

I have noticed that in quite a few countries, such as Turkey, Greece and Mexico, tripe soup is a cure for hangovers, and in Guadalajara most tripe soup restaurants open in the early hours to catch the late-night revellers returning home. I suppose from a British perspective the prospect of a hangover and tripe is frightful, because that's how most people feel about tripe. I, however, find its soft texture and mild flavour particularly comforting and nourishing. A lot depends on how deodorised the tripe has been, as it can smell of bits of the body nobody wants to think about, in much the same way as andouillette, the French pork intestine sausage. Perhaps I should point out that the Mexicans also eat cow's lips, pig's eyeballs, grasshoppers, ants and worms, so tripe is pretty everyday. What I really like about this dish is the addition of the chilli, garlic and cumin paste to the soup just before serving. There's also a salsa verde with toasted chiles de árbol to add to your soup as you wish.

SERVES SIX TO EIGHT

450g tinned hominy
  or 250g dried
2 pig's trotters
1 medium onion,
  peeled and halved
4 cloves garlic
3 bay leaves
1 tsp dried oregano
2 tsp salt
500g bleached honeycomb
  tripe, cleaned and cut
  into 3cm pieces
1 head of celery, sliced
3 tbsp cider vinegar

For the paste
3 guajillo chillies,
  seeds shaken out
3 cloves garlic, peeled
½ tsp cumin
1 tsp salt
100ml cooking liquor

For the salsa verde (optional)
150ml *Stewed salsa verde*
  (page 295)
6 chiles de árbol,
  toasted and ground

To serve
6–8 limes, cut into wedges
Dried oregano
1 onion, chopped

If using dried hominy, soak it overnight in plenty of water, then bring it to the boil and simmer for about 1½ hours.

Put the pig's trotters in a large saucepan with the onion, garlic, bay leaves, oregano and salt. Add 4 litres of water, bring to the boil and skim off any foam that rises to the surface. Simmer for 2 hours, then add the tripe and simmer for a further hour. Top up with water when necessary – you want to end up with about 3 litres of soup.

Remove the trotters with a slotted spoon and when they are cool enough to handle, strip the skin and meat off the bones. Cut it all into 3cm pieces and put it back in the soup. Discard the bones and bay leaves. Add the celery, cider and hominy to the soup and simmer for another 20 minutes.

For the paste, heat a dry, heavy-based frying pan over a medium heat. Toast the chillies for a minute or so on each side until fragrant but not coloured, then put them in a bowl with 300ml of just-boiled water. Leave them for about 20 minutes to soften.

Put the drained chillies in a liquidiser with the garlic, cumin, salt and cooking liquor and blend until smooth. Add this paste to the soup.

Mix the salsa verde with the ground chiles de árbol and put it in a small serving bowl – or offer a bottle of hot sauce like Cholula instead. Serve the soup with the salsa and garnishes on the table so that guests can help themselves.

CHAR-GRILLED VENISON TACOS

Another recipe from chef Miguel Angel Guerrero, the creator of BajaMed Cuisine.
He's happiest when shooting deer and catching trout out in the dry Baha wilderness.
It was one of those times when filming was lost in general great chat and wine but with
a constant outpouring of delicious morsels from his bulbous blue ceramic charcoal grill.
I particularly liked this dish because it's made with quickly grilled venison loin and was
a pleasant change from the slow-cooked meat so loved by Mexicans. There's a recipe
for courgette salad from this great chef on page 128.

SERVES FOUR

600g venison loin
12 x 15cm *corn tortillas*
   (page 44 or bought)
125g cream cheese
200g *Refried beans*
   (page 104)
2 avocados, stoned,
   peeled and sliced
1 lime, cut into wedges

For the dressing
2 shallots, finely chopped
4 cloves garlic,
   finely chopped
3 tbsp olive oil
1 tsp finely chopped thyme
2 tsp finely chopped
   rosemary
Juice of 1 lime

Heat a barbecue and cook the venison loin until medium
rare. The timing will depend on the thickness of the loin
and the heat of your barbecue.

Put it on a board, cover it with foil and leave it to rest
for 5 minutes, then slice into thin strips.

Mix all the ingredients for the dressing, reserving
a teaspoon of the rosemary for the garnish.

Warm the tortillas on the barbecue until softened.
Spread each one with cream cheese and add a spoonful
of refried beans, then top with slices of venison. Add
some of the dressing, a couple of slices of avocado
and a sprinkling of rosemary.

Serve with additional lime wedges.

POSTRES
~ Y ~
BEBIDAS

DESSERTS & DRINKS

Some years ago, I went to Mexico to film a railway journey from Los Mochis, on the Pacific coast of Mexico, to Chihuahua. It was for a series called *Great Railway Journeys*. The route passed through the Copper Canyon, a series of gorges in the Sierra Madre Occidental with vertical copper-green rock sides. It was indeed a great railway journey but not a very long one, so we carried on travelling on Mexican trains through Durango and Zacatecas to Mexico City and then east to Veracruz.

I suppose I have a bit of a one-track mind because what I remember above all was an Aztec soup in Zacatecas and a tlayuda – a crisp open-face tortilla with shredded chicken, avocado and Oaxaca cheese – in Mexico City. Then in El Tajín, an archaeological site near Veracruz, a man approached me from behind an ancient ball court with a bag of chilled orange segments, sprinkled with chilli powder, for sale. They were profoundly refreshing. Maybe it was the recently gained knowledge that the ball court players were often decapitated as an offering to the gods that made the combination so memorable; it seemed to come from an ancient world and introduced me to the idea of fruit and chilli, hence the recipe on page 261 for Mexican fruit salad. This leads me to the pairing of chilli and chocolate, not only in the mole poblano on page 211 of the meat chapter but also in the little chocolate and pasilla fondant truffles on page 274.

This chapter includes recipes for Mexican drinks, like watermelon agua fresca and horchata, both highly refreshing, and some distinguished California cakes like the clementine, almond and olive oil cake on page 282 and Blum's much lauded coffee crunch cake on page 286. But it's the rhubarb galette (page 285) from Chez Panisse in Berkeley that brings back the best memories for me from this latest filming trip. The pastry section was like a film set, the room slightly chilled with wooden worktops for rolling out pastry, and two or three young chefs in immaculate white sorting through rose petals on a tray or piling up clementines, complete with shiny green leaves. One chef was making a delicate rhubarb galette using the first rhubarb of the season with a syrup of some exotic citrus peel and Muscat de Baumes de Venise. In the background some handsome young chefs were sorting through small purple artichokes and Florence fennel. Oh, what it is to be young.

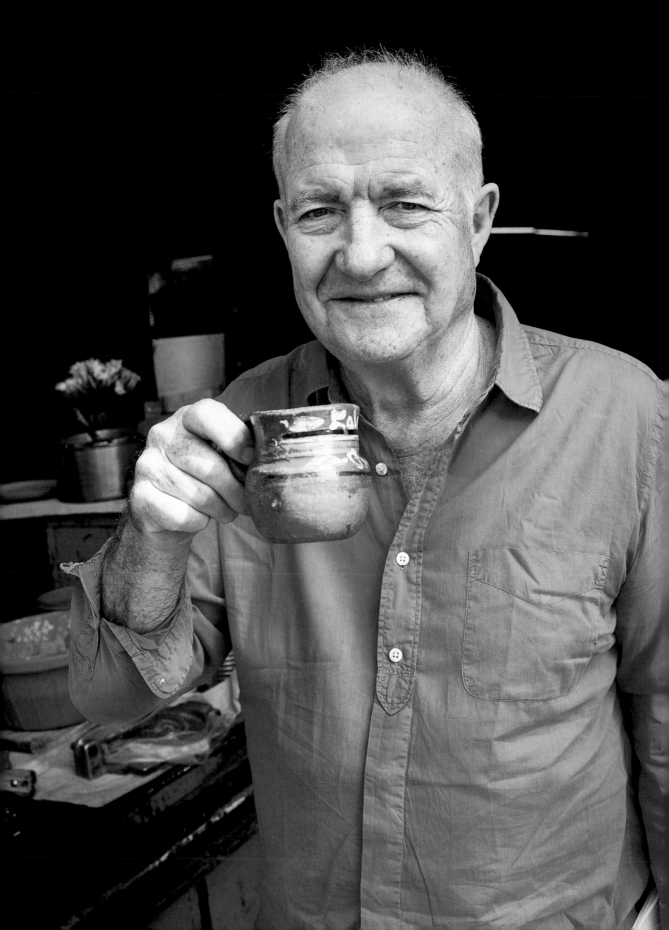

OFERTA
2 KILOS X $ 15

de LO
2X$

OFERTA
3 KILOS X $18

RICE, ALMOND & CINNAMON WATER

A traditional breakfast drink in Mexico, horchata is sold in Cocinas Economicas restaurants and on taco stalls everywhere. It's made with rice, cinnamon and sugar, but there are many variations that include milk or vanilla and almonds, which I've used here as I think they add a nice creaminess to the drink. It's served cold over ice and sprinkled with ground cinnamon. You can replace all or some of the cold water with cow's milk if preferred.

**SERVES FOUR
TO SIX**

200g long-grain white
   rice, uncooked
50g blanched almonds
750ml warm water
3–4cm cinnamon stick,
   broken and crumbled
Pinch ground cinnamon,
   to serve

Syrup
100g white caster sugar

Put the rice and almonds in a bowl with the 750ml of warm water. Add the crumbled cinnamon stick, stir well and cover with cling film. Set aside for at least 6 hours, preferably overnight, at room temperature – do not refrigerate.

Pour the contents of the bowl into a blender and add 450ml of cold water. Blend for 2–3 minutes until as smooth as possible. Line a fine sieve with muslin and strain the liquid into a jug. Discard the ground rice and nuts.

For the syrup, put the sugar in a saucepan with 100ml of water and heat to dissolve the sugar. Bring to the boil and simmer for about 3 minutes, then turn off the heat and allow to cool.

Stir in enough of the syrup to sweeten the horchata to your taste, then chill it well. Serve with ice and sprinkled with a pinch of ground cinnamon.

MEXICAN FRUIT SALAD WITH CHILLI & CACAO NIBS

Outside a school one day, we saw sellers with trays of mango, papaya or pineapple for children to buy as they walked home. The fruit was on sticks and sprinkled with Tajín seasoning (lime, salt and chilli). Children's sweets are often flavoured this way too. This salad is a nod to the sweet, salty, spicy, sour flavours of Mexico and the trick is to use the ripest fruit you can find. You can add strawberries too, if you like. Delicious with yoghurt. *Recipe photograph overleaf*

SERVES EIGHT

2 ripe mangoes, peeled, stoned and diced
¼ watermelon, skin and seeds removed and flesh cut into small wedges
1 small pineapple, peeled, cored and diced
½ cantaloupe melon or a papaya, peeled, deseeded and diced
Juice of 1 orange
Juice of 1 lime
Pinch salt
Pinch hot chilli powder or Tajín seasoning, to taste
3 tbsp raw cacao nibs
Natural yoghurt, to serve (optional)

Mix the fruit in a large bowl, add the orange and lime juice and a pinch of salt, then toss well to combine. Sprinkle with chilli powder or Tajín seasoning and the cacao nibs. Serve with some natural yoghurt if you like.

WATERMELON AGUA FRESCA

Aguas frescas are seen on pretty much every food stall in Mexico, and often a rainbow of different flavours is available. They're made with fresh fruit (bought daily from the market), blended with water and a little sugar and displayed in large barrel dispensers called *vitroleros*, originally made of glass but now plastic. This watermelon flavour is seen all over Mexico and is one of the key colours of the country – a deep pinky red. Very refreshing when served ice cold.

MAKES ABOUT 1.5 LITRES

1.5kg watermelon
1½–2 tbsp caster sugar
Juice of ½ lime

Cut the watermelon into wedges, remove the skin and as many of the big seeds as possible. Cut the melon flesh into cubes and blend in a food processor or blender with 150ml of cold water until smooth. Pass the mixture through a sieve, then stir in the sugar and lime juice to taste.

Pour the agua fresca into a jug and refrigerate. It will separate but just stir it to bring it back together and serve over ice.

SORBETS

I think these three sorbets look fabulous together. The pineapple and lime sorbet and the mango you find on many a menu in the Yucatán. Interestingly, the pineapple often comes with deseeded jalapeño chilli. The hibiscus and orange sorbet was Portia's idea. Both of us noticed how often cafés and restaurants offer hibiscus as a cooling drink. Both agreed it was never quite as satisfying as we hoped it would be. Made into a sorbet with orange, however, hibiscus is a different matter altogether. *Recipe photograph overleaf*

MANGO SORBET

SERVES FOUR
200g caster sugar
Juice of ½ lime
2 large, ripe mangoes,
    peeled, stoned and diced

Put the caster sugar in a pan with 250ml of water and heat until dissolved. Leave it to cool, then add the lime juice.

Put the diced mango in a blender with the sugar syrup and blend until very smooth. Transfer it to an ice-cream maker and churn until soft set. Spoon it into a plastic container and freeze for 3 hours until firm enough to scoop.

HIBISCUS & ORANGE SORBET

SERVES FOUR
40g dried hibiscus flowers
3 or 4 strips of orange zest
    pared with a peeler
200g sugar
Juice of 1 orange
    (about 100ml)

Put the hibiscus flowers and orange zest in a pan with 600ml of water. Bring to the boil, cook for 2 minutes, then turn off the heat and leave to steep for about 20 minutes.

Strain the liquid into a clean pan and add the sugar. Heat slowly to dissolve the sugar and then bring to the boil, turn off the heat and leave to cool. Add the orange juice.

Once the liquid is cool, pour it into an ice-cream maker and churn until slushy. Spoon it into a plastic container and freeze for 3 hours until firm enough to scoop.

PINEAPPLE & LIME SORBET

SERVES FOUR
1 medium, ripe pineapple,
    peeled, cored and chopped
    (about 400g prepared
    pineapple chunks)
50g caster sugar
Zest and juice of 1 lime
1 jalapeño chilli, deseeded
    and finely chopped
    (optional)

Put the pineapple chunks and any juice with the sugar, lime zest and juice and 125ml of water into a blender and process to a smooth purée. Stir in the chopped jalapeño, if using. Pour the mixture into an ice-cream maker and churn to sorbet consistency. Scoop the purée into a plastic container and freeze for 2–3 hours or more before serving.

RICK'S MARGARITA

I spent half a day in the town of Tequila at a boutique distillery called Fortaleza. Every town needs to have something it's famous for. Monterey in California is known for John Steinbeck's novel *Cannery Row,* and near the town of Nambour on the Sunshine Coast of Queensland there's a monument to the tropical fruit growing all around called The Big Pineapple. But perhaps nowhere has such a success story as Tequila. For miles around, there are fields of beautiful blue-grey agave plants, and when you get to the town it's one historic distillery with noble oak doors after another. Jose Cuervo and Sauza are the two giants in Tequila but Fortaleza is the special one – small production and everything done by hand. The bottle itself is a work of art, with its distinctive cork made in the shape of the agave heart, the piña. To celebrate tequila, I asked Ryan Chetiyawardana, the king of cocktails in London and winner of International Bartender of the Year, to come up with a super margarita for our restaurants. Normally a margarita is one third tequila, one third Cointreau and one third fresh lime juice. This is what Ryan had to say: 'A margarita is best served blisteringly cold, and the best examples are shaken so vigorously that the aeration lends a pleasing foam to the drink. It needs this to help with the balance, and although my measurements are a little trickier than equal parts, this gives a nuance that will really elevate the classic combination. The Tajín gives a piquant salinity that contrasts the flavours wonderfully'. He adds a slice of mango dipped in Tajín seasoning, which is chilli powder, dehydrated lime juice and salt, to the cocktail. The other point he makes is that using tequila made with 100% agave like Fortaleza will be a revelation. Most popular tequilas are a mixture of grain spirit and tequila.

SERVES ONE
45ml 100% agave
    blanco tequila
25ml Cointreau
20ml freshly squeezed
    lime juice
Slice of mango
Tajín seasoning

Shake the tequila, Cointreau and lime juice very hard over a full shaker of cubed ice until the shaker is frosted. Double strain into a chilled cocktail glass, without ice, and garnish with the slice of mango dipped in Tajín seasoning.

CAJETA
GOAT'S MILK CARAMEL

Goat's milk cajeta, like cow's milk dulce de leche, is very popular in Mexico and is delicious served with ice cream, for dipping churros, or drizzled over crêpes. It has the distinctive Mexican flavours of cinnamon and vanilla and you can add a some sea salt flakes if you like a salted caramel. Serve with vanilla ice cream (page 299).

**SERVES SIX
TO EIGHT**
1 litre goat's milk
200g granulated sugar
1 vanilla pod, split open
5cm cinnamon stick
½ tsp bicarbonate of soda
Sea salt flakes (optional)

In a large pan, with at least a 3-litre capacity, heat the goat's milk and sugar over a low to medium heat. Keep stirring until the sugar is dissolved, then add the vanilla pod, along with its scraped-out seeds, and the cinnamon stick and bring to the boil. Take the pan off the heat and immediately add the bicarbonate of soda. Everything will fizz and bubble up briefly, but stir well and once it subsides, put the pan back over the heat.

Turn the heat down to a simmer and cook, stirring regularly, for 50 minutes to an hour, until the mixture has turned a deep golden caramel colour. You must keep stirring or the mixture will catch and burn on the bottom of the pan.

Once the mixture has reached the consistency of double cream and is a deep golden colour, remove the pan from the heat. Let it cool slightly, then taste and add sea salt flakes, if desired. Pour into a sterilised jar.

If not using the cajeta straight away, let it cool completely, then store it in the fridge for up to two weeks. It will thicken on cooling so if you need to soften it for later use as a sauce, spoon it into a pan and heat it gently. You can loosen it with a little hot water or goat's milk if necessary.

PAN DE ELOTE
SWEETCORN MUFFINS

It's simply the sweetcorn that makes these muffins so special. Well, that and the condensed milk. These are highly recommended with your afternoon cup of tea. If you like, you can bake the mixture in one tin as a traybake.

MAKES EIGHTEEN MUFFINS

100g butter, melted,
  plus extra for greasing
500g frozen sweetcorn,
  defrosted in a sieve,
  or fresh kernels cut
  from 4 good-sized cobs
397g tin of condensed milk
1 tsp vanilla extract
¼ tsp salt
3 eggs
100g plain flour
2 tsp baking powder

Preheat the oven to 180°C/Fan 160°C. Generously butter 18 holes of a couple of non-stick muffin tins. Alternatively, use a baking tin measuring about 35 x 20cm.

Tip 400g of the corn into a food processor, add the condensed milk, vanilla extract, salt and melted butter and process until fairly smooth. Add the eggs, one at a time, processing between each addition, then add the flour, baking powder and the remaining 100g of corn kernels, still whole.

Pour the mixture into the greased muffin tins or the baking tray. Bake in the preheated oven for 25–30 minutes for muffins or 40–50 minutes for the traybake. Cook until the top is golden and a skewer comes out clean.

Leave the muffins to cool slightly and if you've made a traybake, cut into about 18 squares. Serve warm or cold with vanilla ice cream (page 299) or a cup of tea.

CHOCOLATE & PASILLA FONDANT TRUFFLES

These are addictive. Pasilla chillies are dried and have a gorgeous fruitiness about them, so this combination of chocolate, a hint of fruit and not too hot chilli makes for a great treat. The recipe calls for the truffles to be dipped in batter and fried just long enough to make them crisp on the outside but still slightly gooey inside. Alternatively, if you just refrigerate them and don't add the batter, you have petits fours to go with coffee.

MAKES FIFTEEN TO EIGHTEEN

1 large pasilla chilli
    or 4 tsp ground pasilla
200ml double cream
⅛ tsp, or more to taste,
    cayenne pepper (optional)
Pinch salt
200g dark chocolate
    (70% cocoa solids),
    chopped into small pieces
6 heaped tbsp cocoa
    powder, for dusting
1 litre corn oil,
    for deep frying

For the batter
120g plain flour
1½ tbsp caster sugar
1 tsp baking powder
Pinch salt
1 egg
100ml ice-cold water
    or milk (water yields
    a crisper batter coating)

To serve
Whipped or clotted cream
250g small strawberries
    or raspberries

If using a whole chilli, toast it for about 10 seconds on each side in a dry pan, then grind to a powder in a spice grinder.

Heat the cream in a pan with the ground pasilla, cayenne, if using, and the salt. When the cream is hot but not boiling, take the pan off the heat and add the chocolate to the cream. Stir gently until the chocolate has melted. Set aside to cool and then chill until it is firm enough to shape into balls.

Using two teaspoons, shape the chocolate into 15–18 small lozenges and drop them into a bowl of cocoa powder. Using your hands and working quickly so as not to melt the chocolate, roll them into balls, dusting them with cocoa powder as you go. Put them on a tray lined with baking parchment and freeze for at least 3 hours, preferably overnight. Once frozen, they can be kept for a week or two if you like. Store them layered with baking parchment in a plastic box with a lid.

Ten minutes before you are ready to finish the truffles, make the batter. Sift the flour, sugar, baking powder and salt into a bowl, make a well in the centre and add the egg. Whisk the egg, gradually drawing in the flour from the sides to make a paste. Add the water or milk a little at a time until you have a smooth, thick batter.

Heat the oil to 175°C in a large saucepan. Dip the frozen truffles into the batter, lower them into the hot oil and fry for a couple of minutes until golden. Do this in batches, setting each batch aside on kitchen paper.

Trim off any ragged batter edges with scissors if you like. Serve immediately dusted with cocoa powder and with whipped or clotted cream and some red berries on the side.

MEXICAN HOT CHOCOLATE

When you order 'chocolate caliente' in Mexico you will usually be asked if you want it made with water or milk. It is a quite different (albeit delicious) drink made with water, but with milk it is more akin to what we are used to. Mayordomo is a brand of chocolate sold all over Mexico and already contains ground cinnamon, so if you are lucky enough to get some over here, you won't need to add any to the drink. Hot chocolate is popular all over Mexico but especially in Oaxaca, where it is frothed with a wooden swizzle stick called a *molinillo*.

SERVES TWO TO THREE

550ml semi-skimmed milk (or water)

100g dark chocolate, 70% cocoa solids, chopped

1 tsp demerara sugar (to taste)

½ tsp ground cinnamon (or infuse milk with cinnamon stick)

Heat 150ml of the milk in a saucepan and add the chopped chocolate, sugar and the cinnamon, if using. Whisk until the chocolate has melted and the mixture is smooth. Add the remaining milk and continue to heat until it's hot but not boiling, then serve.

CHOCOLATE MARTINI

This, as my friend Mark Knight Adams says of such frivolous things, is a little bit of nonsense. It's from the Casa Kimberly Hotel in Puerta Vallarta, which was originally the home of Elizabeth Taylor and Richard Burton, and it was Elizabeth's favourite cocktail.

SERVES ONE

¼ orange

1 tsp cocoa powder

50ml vodka

25ml crème de cacao liqueur

25ml chocolate syrup

Handful of ice

Rub the rim of a martini glass with the quarter of orange. Sprinkle the cocoa powder on to a saucer, then dip the rim of the glass into the cocoa to coat.

Pour the vodka, crème de cacao and chocolate syrup into a cocktail shaker with ice and shake well. Strain into the prepared glass and serve.

BUÑUELOS WITH SPICED GUAVA SYRUP

In Guadalajara, buñuelos, which are deep-fried wheat pancakes, are known as Buñuelos Santuario, because the stalls that sell them are right next door to a very beautiful church called the Santuario de Virgen de Guadalupe. Buñuelos occur in many different forms all over Spain and Latin America and traditionally the flat ones were shaped over your knee. These days they arrive at the stands ready-fried. When you order, they're crushed into a bowl and hot cinnamon- and guava-flavoured syrup is poured over the top. They are completely delicious and, as with many a Mexican dish (such as ahogados on page 62), it is the combination of softness and crispness that makes them so satisfying. I cooked some the other night for friends and served them with a dollop of ice cream and I'm thinking of doing them in the restaurant. Desserts are so pretty these days it would be nice to get something rugged and Mexican out there for a change. *Recipe photograph overleaf*

**SERVES SIX
TO EIGHT**

For the buñuelos
300g plain flour
1 tsp baking powder
1 tbsp caster sugar
½ tsp salt
1 egg, lightly beaten
1 tsp vanilla extract
15g butter, melted
125–150ml tepid water
700ml corn or vegetable
    oil, for frying

*For the guava or
    mango syrup*
300g brown sugar
8cm cinnamon stick
2 strips orange peel, pared
    with a potato peeler
1 star anise
4 allspice berries
Pinch salt
Juice of 1 lime
Juice of 1 orange
1 tsp cornflour, mixed to a
    paste with 1 tbsp water
350g guavas, quartered,
    or 350g mango, peeled,
    stoned and cut into
    4–5cm chunks

Put all the dry ingredients for the buñuelos in a large bowl. Make a well in the centre and add the egg, vanilla and melted butter, then stir until the mixture resembles coarse breadcrumbs. Add the water, about one-quarter at a time, and mix to a smooth dough. Knead for about 5 minutes on a floured board, then cover the dough with a tea towel and leave it to rest for 30 minutes.

For the fruit syrup, put the sugar, cinnamon, orange peel, star anise, allspice and salt in a pan with 1 litre of water and the lime and orange juice. Stir until the sugar has dissolved, then bring to a boil and simmer for about 20 minutes. Add the cornflour mixture and stir until it has thickened the syrup. Add the guava or mango and cook for another 15 minutes until tender.

Heat the oil for the buñuelos in a frying pan to 190°C or until a cube of bread browns in 30 seconds. Divide the dough into 6–8 balls and roll each one out into a 2mm-thick round like a tortilla. It should able to fit into your frying pan. Fry each round until golden and crisp on one side, then flip it over and cook the other side. Remove and drain on kitchen paper, then sprinkle with cinnamon sugar. Repeat to cook the rest.

Break the buñuelos up roughly and serve them in bowls, with a ladle of the syrup and fruit chunks ladled over the top.

CLEMENTINE, ALMOND & OLIVE OIL CAKE

This cake is a celebration of California citrus fruit. After the gold rush, the prosperity of this state, the largest economy in the Union, came from the massive cultivation of oranges. Californians treat citrus in the same way as the British view apples. They know all the many varieties and shop for them by taste and name. To honour this, we filmed at a family citrus farm just outside Ojai in Ventura County, east of Santa Barbara. The owners, Jim Churchill and his wife Lisa Brenneis, were picking Pixie tangerines and Kishu mandarins and I ate them straight off the tree. Not being used to picking tangerines off the tree, it was a bit of an emotional moment for me. You can use any kind of small citrus fruit for this cake.

SERVES EIGHT

2 large clementines
  (about 200g), scrubbed
4 large eggs
Zest of 1 large lemon
160g caster sugar
100ml olive oil
175g ground almonds
2 tsp baking powder
Icing or caster sugar,
  for dusting

For the syrup
15g caster sugar
Juice of 1 large lemon

To serve (optional)
250ml whipped cream
2–3 oranges, segmented

Put the whole clementines in a saucepan and cover them with water. Bring to the boil and simmer gently for 20–30 minutes until the tangerines are tender. Remove them and set aside until cool enough to handle. Cut the fruit in half and, with the tip of a knife, remove and discard the pips. Put the skin and pulp in a food processor and blend to a paste.

Preheat the oven to 180°C/Fan 160°C. Grease a 20cm springform cake tin and line the bottom with baking parchment. Whisk the eggs, lemon zest and caster sugar in a bowl. Add the olive oil and beat until light and well combined. Add the clementine paste and stir, then fold in the ground almonds and baking powder.

Spoon the mixture into the prepared tin. Bake for about 50 minutes or until well risen and golden. The cake should have slightly shrunken from the sides and be springy to the touch. Leave it to cool in the tin on a wire rack while you make the syrup.

Warm the sugar and lemon juice in a small pan until the sugar has dissolved. Make lots of small holes all over the cake with a piece of uncooked spaghetti and drizzle over the lemon syrup. Let the cake cool completely in the tin, then turn it out on to a serving plate. Dust with icing sugar and serve with whipped cream and orange segements if you like.

RHUBARB GALETTE CHEZ PANISSE

Going to Chez Panisse was inevitably a high point of California for me. Alice Waters at Chez Panisse has for years been my ideal – she runs a small local restaurant serving what's fresh from the market and with a menu that changes every day – and meeting her only reinforced that. I've chosen the rhubarb galette from the many dishes I tasted. The restaurant's pastry section is the sort of place you'd love your teenager to work, surrounded by Californian citrus fruit, baskets of rose petals and the new season's rhubarb. Would that every youngster aspiring to become a chef could join such a kitchen. I did ask Alice if my stepdaughter Olivia could do a stage there. And she said yes.

SERVES EIGHT

225g plain flour
Pinch salt
170g cold, unsalted butter,
    cut into 1cm cubes
80ml ice-cold water

For the filling
500g rhubarb, cut
    into 6cm long batons
    (save any trimmings)
Finely grated zest
    of an orange
200g granulated sugar
Pinch salt
Juice ½ orange
1 tbsp muscat dessert wine
30g unsalted butter, melted
30g caster sugar
2 tbsp sugar, for the glaze

To serve
Vanilla ice cream (page 299)
    or whipped cream

In a food processor, pulse the flour and salt. Add the butter and process briefly. Sprinkle over the ice-cold water and pulse for about 5 seconds, until just moistened.

Transfer the dough to a floured work surface and knead it 2 or 3 times until it comes together. Pat the dough into a disc. Lay a sheet of baking parchment on your work surface and dust it with flour. Roll out the dough like a pizza to make a 35cm circle, 4–5mm thick. Transfer the parchment to a baking sheet and chill the pastry.

Preheat the oven to 220°C/Fan 200°C. Toss the rhubarb in a bowl with the orange zest, sugar, salt, juice and wine and mix well. Arrange the rhubarb on top of the pastry and sprinkle over any remaining sugary mixture. Leave a border of 5–6cm around the edge of the pastry, fold that in and crimp to form a border. Brush the fruit with melted butter and sprinkle with caster sugar, then repeat this process three times.

Bake the galette for 10–12 minutes, then lower the oven temperature to 200°C/Fan 180°C and bake for a further 30–35 minutes.

To make the glaze, cook the rhubarb trimmings with 75ml of water until soft. Strain the liquid from the pulp and add the 2 tablespoons of sugar. Pour this back into the pan and let the sugar dissolve, then reduce to a thick syrup.

Leave the galette to cool, then brush it with the glaze. Serve with vanilla ice cream or whipped cream.

BLUM'S COFFEE CRUNCH CAKE

This is from the famous Blum's bakery in San Francisco. It's all about texture –
the lightness of the sponge and the whipped cream icing with the crunchy topping.

SERVES TWELVE
Vegetable oil, for greasing
175g self-raising flour
½ tsp salt
300g caster sugar
6 eggs, separated
1 tsp cream of tartar
1 tsp vanilla extract
1 tbsp lemon juice
1 tsp grated lemon zest

For the coffee crunch topping
Vegetable oil, for greasing
1 tbsp bicarbonate of soda
60ml strong espresso coffee
250g caster or
    granulated sugar
4 tbsp golden syrup

For the icing/filling
500ml double cream
2 tsp vanilla extract
2 tbsp icing sugar, sifted

Preheat the oven to 180°C/Fan 160°C. Grease a loose-bottomed 23cm cake tin and line it with baking parchment.

Sift the flour with the salt and 150g of the sugar on to greaseproof paper and set aside. With an electric whisk, beat the egg yolks with 50g of the sugar until pale and creamy. Add 60ml of water and continue to whisk for about 4 minutes until thickened.

Whisk the egg whites in a large bowl until frothy. Add the cream of tartar and continue to whisk to soft peak stage. Add 100g caster sugar in a steady stream and whisk until the mixture forms thick stiff, glossy peaks, then add the vanilla, lemon juice and zest and whisk to combine.

Pour the egg yolk mixture into the bowl with the egg whites and fold together, keeping as much air in as possible. Add the sifted flour and sugar, one-third at a time, folding it in carefully after each addition. Pour the mixture into the tin and bake in the bottom third of the oven for 50–55 minutes until well risen, golden and slightly shrinking from the sides. Cool in the tin on a wire rack, then run a knife around the sides and turn the cake out on to the rack. Using a bread knife, cut the cake horizontally into 3 tiers.

While the cake cools, make the topping. Grease a baking sheet. Sift the bicarb on to a piece of baking parchment. Put the coffee, sugar and syrup into a large pan and stir over a low heat until the sugar has dissolved. Turn up the heat and cook to 145°C – check with a jam thermometer.

When the mixture is up to temperature, take the pan off the heat and add the bicarbonate of soda. Stir well while it froths and foams, then immediately pour the mixture on to the baking sheet and leave it to set for about an hour. When it's cool, break it into chunks, then put it in a food bag and smash into pieces with a rolling pin. Store in an airtight tin until ready to use.

To make the icing, whip the double cream until it forms soft peaks, then fold in the vanilla and icing sugar. Assemble the cake, spreading each layer with the whipped cream. Spread the top and sides with cream and smooth them with a palette knife, then put the cake in the fridge. Serve sprinkled with plenty of the topping.

MEXICAN RICE PUDDING WITH HONEYCOMB

I like the way that in Mexico the rice for rice pudding is first cooked in water. Even though the cooked rice is then mixed with milk and condensed milk, the rice still tastes clean and not claggy. This is common everywhere, but I once had a rice pudding with a sprinkling of honeycomb on the top which I found particularly satisfying. I also like the typically Mexican flavouring of cinnamon and vanilla.

SERVES SIX TO EIGHT

225g short-grain (pudding) rice
5cm cinnamon stick
550ml whole milk
250ml condensed milk
1 tsp vanilla extract

For the honeycomb
10g butter
75g golden syrup
200g caster sugar
2 tsp bicarbonate of soda

To serve
½ tsp ground cinnamon, for sprinkling
2 ripe mangoes, peeled, stoned and cut into slivers

Make the honeycomb first. Grease a baking tray with the butter and set it aside. Put the golden syrup and caster sugar in a large saucepan and let it dissolve over a low heat until you can't see the sugar crystals. Turn up the heat and cook until the mixture is a deep caramel colour. Turn off the heat and immediately add the bicarbonate of soda. Stir to mix well while it bubbles and foams, then pour the mixture on to the greased baking tray and leave it to cool for 1–1½ hours. Break it into shards and store in an airtight container between sheets of baking parchment for up to a week.

Put the rice in a sieve, wash it well under cold running water, then drain. Tip the rice into a saucepan, add the cinnamon stick and 700ml of water, then bring to the boil. Cover the pan, turn the heat down and cook slowly for 10–15 minutes until the rice is tender. Most of the water should have been absorbed, but if not drain it away and discard. Remove the cinnamon stick.

Add the milk and condensed milk to the pan with the rice and stir to combine. Bring to the boil, then lower the heat and cook gently for 5–7 minutes until the rice is fairly thick and creamy. Stir in the vanilla extract. Remove the pan from the heat and leave it to stand for 5 minutes.

Serve hot or cold, sprinkled with ground cinnamon, shards of honeycomb and slivers of mango. If you're serving the pudding hot, the honeycomb will melt into the rice very quickly, so it's better to offer it separately at the table.

STAPLES

STEWED SALSA VERDE

SERVES FOUR

380g tinned tomatillos, drained
1–2 green jalapeño or
   serrano chillies, sliced
½ onion, chopped
1 clove garlic, sliced
¼ tsp salt
¼ tsp caster sugar
1 large handful coriander, chopped
Juice of ½ lime, to taste

Put the drained tomatillos in a saucepan
with 2 or 3 tablespoons of water. Add the
chopped chillies, onion, garlic, salt and
sugar and bring to the boil. Turn the heat
down to a simmer and stew for about
20 minutes until the mixture has softened,
adding a little more water if it looks as
though it is drying out. Check the onions
and cook for another 5 minutes if they
need to soften more.

Add three-quarters of the coriander
and the lime juice to taste – tomatillos
can be quite tart so add the lime a
little at time. Pulse in a food processor
until pulpy, then garnish with the
remaining coriander.

ROASTED TOMATILLO SALSA

SERVES FOUR TO SIX

10 tomatillos, husks removed
2 cloves garlic, skin on
1–2 green jalapeño
   or serrano chillies
¼ tsp salt
1 small onion, finely chopped
1 small handful fresh
   coriander, chopped
Juice of ½ lime

On a barbecue, in a heavy-based pan or
under a grill, grill the tomatillos, garlic
and chillies until they are softened and
have some charred patches. Remove
and set aside.

When everything is cool enough to handle,
roughly chop the tomatillos, peel the garlic
and remove the stems from the chillies
(and the seeds if you want a milder salsa).

Pound the garlic and chillies in a pestle
and mortar and when they're broken up,
add the tomatillos and the salt. Continue
to pound until you have a rich thick pulpy
salsa. You can do this in a food processor
if you prefer a smoother salsa. Stir in the
chopped onion and coriander, then add
lime juice to taste.

PINK PICKLED ONIONS

MAKES 1 X 500ML JAR

3 medium-sized red onions,
    halved and thinly sliced
60ml cider vinegar
Juice of ½ orange
Juice of 1 lime
½ tsp sea salt
1 habanero chilli (optional)

Soak the red onion slices in a bowl of just-boiled water for 10 minutes, then drain and discard the water. Add the remaining ingredients, except the chilli, if using, and toss well to mix.

Pack it all into a clean glass jar and add a little more orange juice if needed to cover the onion slices. If using the habanero, wash it and cut a small slit in the flesh, then push it into the liquid.

Seal the jar and put it in the fridge for at least 4 hours, preferably overnight, before using. Serve with tacos and meat dishes.

GUACATILLO SAUCE

SERVES FOUR TO SIX

6 tomatillos, fresh or tinned
2 large, ripe avocados, stoned and peeled
½ onion, very roughly chopped
1–2 green jalapeño or serrano chillies
A small handful of coriander
1 garlic clove, peeled and bashed
Juice of 1 lime
½ tsp salt

If using tinned tomatillos, drain them. Put all the ingredients in a blender and whizz to a smooth sauce. Add a little more lime juice or water if needed to get the desired consistency. Serve with tacos, salads, tostadas and so on.

HOT RED CHILLI SAUCE

MAKES ABOUT 400ML

15 chiles de árbol, stems removed,
    seeds shaken out
4 guajillo chillies, stems removed,
    seeds shaken out
3 cloves garlic
2 tomatoes, quartered
80ml cider vinegar
½ tsp ground cumin
4 allspice berries, ground or a good
    pinch of ground allspice
1 tsp dried oregano
1 tsp salt
1 tbsp light brown sugar

Toast the chillies in a hot dry frying pan for a few minutes until fragrant. Put them in a saucepan, add the garlic and 700ml of water, then bring to the boil and simmer for 15 minutes. Keep the window open or the extractor running when cooking the chillies as this really is spicy! Take the pan off the heat and allow the chillies to cool a little.

Put the chillies, garlic and 250ml of their cooking water in a blender. Add the tomatoes, vinegar, cumin, allspice, oregano, salt and sugar and blend to a fine a sauce as possible. If necessary, strain the sauce through a sieve if it is still coarse in texture.

Pour the sauce into a clean pan and cook for 5–7 minutes over a medium-high heat until it is reduced and thickened slightly. Pour it through a funnel into sterilised glass bottle or jar and seal. It keeps for about 3 months in the fridge. This is a very hot sauce and good for splashing over anything from chilaquiles (page 24) to chips.

PICO DE GALLO SALSA

ENOUGH FOR FOUR TO SIX WITH TACOS AND TOSTADAS OR AS A DIP WITH TOTOPOS

2 large ripe tomatoes, deseeded
    and finely diced
½ onion, finely chopped
A handful of coriander, chopped
1 green serrano or jalapeño chilli,
    finely chopped
¼ tsp salt
Juice of ½ –1 lime

Mix all the ingredients in a bowl, starting with juice of half a lime and adding more to taste, if desired. Serve immediately.

CHIPOTLE CREMA

SERVES TWO TO FOUR

2 *Chipotles en adobo*, finely chopped
    or mashed in a pestle and mortar
2 tbsp soured cream
2 tbsp mayonnaise
Squeeze of lime juice
Pinch of salt

Mix all the ingredients together and set aside.

CHIPOTLES EN ADOBO

MAKES ENOUGH FOR A 370G JAR

8 chipotle chillies
3 large ripe tomatoes, roughly chopped
1 medium onion, roughly chopped
4 large cloves garlic, peeled and sliced
60ml cider vinegar
¾ tsp salt
2 tsp brown sugar

Wash the chillies, remove the hard stems, but leave the seeds in place. Put the chillies in a bowl with 150ml of just-boiled water and cover with cling film. Leave the chillies to soak for about 20 minutes.

Remove 3 of the soaked chipotles, leaving the rest in the water, and put them in a food processor or blender. Add the tomatoes, onion, garlic, cider vinegar, salt, the soaking liquid and the sugar, then process to make a smooth paste.

Tip this paste into a pan and add the remaining whole soaked chipotles.

Bring to the boil, then reduce the heat and simmer the chipotles for about 1 hour. Check them every 20–30 minutes and add a little more boiling water if needed.

Leave to cool slightly, then pour into a sterilised glass jar. Cool completely and store in the fridge for up to a month.

TOTOPOS & TORTILLA STRIPS

SERVES FOUR TO SIX WITH DIPS

6–8 x 15cm *Corn tortillas* (page 44),
　each cut into 6 wedges, like a pizza
1 litre corn or vegetable oil
Pinch salt

For totopos, heat the oil to 190°C in a large pan and cook the tortilla triangles in small batches until barely golden and crisp. Using a slotted spoon, transfer them to a plate lined with kitchen paper to drain. Sprinkle with a little salt.

Serve as soon as possible with dips, in chilaquiles (page 24) or with soup or stew.

To make tortilla strips to use in soup or stew, follow the method above but instead of cutting the tortillas into triangles, cut them into strips 1cm wide.

MAYONNAISE

MAKES 300ML

2 egg yolks
1 tbsp English mustard (not powder)
1 tbsp white wine vinegar
¾ tsp salt
300ml sunflower oil

Make sure all the ingredients are at room temperature before beginning.

Put everything except the oil in a mixing bowl. Using a wire whisk, beat in the oil a little at a time until it is all incorporated. Once you have added about a quarter of the oil you can add the rest more quickly.

VANILLA ICE CREAM

SERVES SIX

300ml milk
300ml double cream
1 vanilla pod
6cm cinnamon stick
6 egg yolks
125g caster sugar

Pour the milk and cream into a saucepan. Split the vanilla pod lengthways and scrape the black seeds into the pan, then add the pod and the cinnamon stick. Bring the mixture almost to boiling point and then take the pan off the heat and allow the vanilla pod and cinnamon to infuse for about half an hour.

Whisk the egg yolks in a bowl with the sugar until pale and fluffy. Remove the vanilla pod and cinnamon stick, then slowly whisk the mixture into the egg yolks and sugar. Pour this custard into a clean pan.

Put the pan of custard over a low to medium heat and heat, stirring continually with a wooden spoon, until it's thick enough to coat the back of the spoon. Do not allow it to boil or you will end up with a scrambled egg mixture. Remove the pan from the heat, pour the custard into a cold bowl and leave it to cool. Then refrigerate until cold before pouring it into an ice-cream maker until almost frozen.

If you don't have an ice-cream maker, pour the mixture into a plastic box and freeze it for an hour. Remove it from the freezer and, using a fork, work from the edges to break up any crystals that have formed. Repeat this 3 times to prevent a granular texture, then freeze the ice cream for about 3 hours until it's firm enough to scoop.

CHICKEN STOCK

MAKES ABOUT 1.75 LITRES

Bones from a 1.5kg chicken or
    45g wings/drumsticks or leftover
    bones from a roasted chicken
1 large carrot, roughly chopped
2 celery sticks, roughly chopped
2 leeks, sliced
2 bay leaves
2 sprigs thyme
2.25 litres water
1 tsp salt

Put all the ingredients in a large pan and bring to the boil, skimming any scum from the surface. Leave to simmer very gently for 2 hours. It is important not to let the stock boil as that emulsifies the fat from the chicken and makes the stock cloudy.

    Strain the stock through a sieve, then simmer a little linger to concentrate the flavour if necessary. If not using the stock immediately, leave it to cool, then chill or freeze for later use.

SHELLFISH STOCK

MAKES ABOUT 1 LITRE

You can make this with the heads and shells of prawns, crabs, lobsters or langoustines, or with whole shell-on North Atlantic prawns.

50ml olive oil
200g shells or whole prawns
1 medium onion, chopped
2 cloves garlic, chopped
40g tomato purée
3 tomatoes, chopped
75ml white wine
1 tsp oregano
1 tsp salt
½ tsp chilli flakes
800ml fish stock (right) or water

Heat the oil in a big saucepan and stir-fry the shells or whole prawns, onion and garlic for 5 minutes. Add the rest of the ingredients, bring to the boil and simmer gently for 1 hour. Remove any hard thick bits of shell, like crab or lobster claws. Blitz the rest in a blender or food processor, then pass the stock through a sieve.

FISH STOCK

MAKES ABOUT 1.25 LITRES

Using 500g cheap white fish fillet (such as whiting or coley) cut into 2cm slices, instead of bones, gives this stock a richer flavour, but use whatever you have.

1 onion chopped
1 bulb fennel, sliced
100g celery, sliced
100g carrots, sliced
25g button mushrooms, washed and sliced
Sprig thyme
2.25 litres water
1 tsp salt
1kg flatfish bones (such as brill, sole, plaice),
    or 500g fillet

Put all the ingredients, except the fish bones or fillet, into a large pan and bring to the boil. Then turn down the heat and simmer gently for 20 minutes.

    Add the fish bones or fillet and bring back up to a simmer, skimming off any scum as it rises to the surface. Simmer for a further 20 minutes. Strain through a sieve into a clean pan and simmer a little longer, if necessary, until reduced to about 1.25 litres. If not using the stock immediately, leave it to cool, then chill or freeze for later use.

INGREDIENTS

CHILLIES

The chillies used in this book vary in heat intensity from the mild poblano to the very hot habanero. I would recommend anyone with sensitive skin to use gloves when handling hot chillies like habaneros. To reduce the heat of a chilli, remove the seeds and the placental membrane that surrounds them. This is easily done with a teaspoon. The seeds themselves have no capsaicin, the hot stuff, but the membrane contains the greatest concentration in the fruit.

DRIED CHILLIES

Dried chillies are usually briefly toasted in a dry pan and rehydrated in just-boiled water for about 20 minutes prior to use.

ANCHO
A dried poblano chilli, this is often rehydrated and stuffed, or used in mole sauces. About 3/10 on the heat scale.

ARBOL
This small hot red chilli is particularly good in hot sauces. About 8/10 on the heat scale.

CHIPOTLE 'MORITA'
A dried and smoked jalapeño, dark brown to black in colour, this gives a deep smoky flavour to salsas and stews. About 6–7/10 on the heat scale.

GUAJILLO
A very widely used, smooth-skinned, deep dark-brown chilli. About 3/10 on the heat scale.

MULATO
A darker skinned version of the ancho, this ripens to dark brown and black when dried. About 3/10 on the heat scale.

PASILLA
A dried chilaca chilli with a fruity flavour, this is used extensively in stews and sauces. About 4/10 on the heat scale,

FRESH CHILLIES

HABANERO
A hot chilli, these can be red, green or orange and are favoured in the Yucatán region. About 9/10 on the heat scale.

JALAPEÑO
Usually used when green (but occasionally red) and often added to salsas, tacos and burritos. I recommend red, ripened, jalapeños in a few recipes, as they are slightly sweeter and hotter than the green, but if you can't find them it's fine to use green. Heat can vary quite a bit from chilli to chilli but generally about 4/10 on the heat scale.

POBLANO
The mildest of chillies, these are large and waxy-skinned with dark-green flesh. Used for stuffing or cut into strips for rajas (page 114). About 1/10 on the heat scale but increases to 3/10 when ripened to a deep red.

SERRANO
Usually used green, these chillies are widely used in salsas in Mexican cuisine. They are not always easy to find in the UK so often substituted in this book with jalapeños. About 5/10 on the heat scale.

MEXICAN LARDER

STORE CUPBOARD

ACHIOTE PASTE
A paste made with annatto seeds ground with salt, garlic and spices.

BLACK TURTLE BEANS
These are available dried or tinned and used to make refried beans.

BLUE CORN TORTILLA FLOUR
The blue maize version of maize flour (see below).

CHIPOTLES IN ADOBO
Chipotle chillies in a tomato and garlic sauce. Make your own (page 298) or buy in tins from Mexican food suppliers (page 308).

HOMINY GRAIN,
Nixtamalised whole corn, available dried or tinned.

HOT SAUCE
Brands include Cholula, Huichol and Tabasco or see page 296.

MAIZE FLOUR
Ground maize, known as masa harina, used to make masa dough for tortillas. It is finely ground for tortillas and more coarsely milled for tamales. It is not the same as UK cornflour and needs to be sourced from Mexican suppliers (see suppliers page 308).

PINTO BEANS
An alternative to black beans, often used for making refried beans.

TAJÍN SEASONING
A mix of chilli powder, salt and dried powdered lime.

TAMAL MASA FLOUR
This is coarser ground than masa harina and used to make tamales which are like steamed dumplings, stuffed with a savoury, or sweet, filling.

TOMATILLOS
These firm-freshed green fruits are related to tomatoes and can be green, yellow or purple. Fresh tomatillos are not widely available in the UK but tinned tomatillos work very well in salsas (see suppliers page 308).

FRESH PRODUCE

EPAZOTE
A green herb with a pungent, some say slightly petrol-like, flavour. Available dried. You can use oregano as an alternative. It's not really the same taste but it gives a resinous herbal note to a dish.

HOJA SANTA
Large-leafed green herb used in Central and Southern Mexico, particularly for pozole. I think its complex flavour is most similar to tarragon or possibly fennel.

MEXICAN CHEESES
Most often used are Cojita and Oaxacan stringy cheese. In the UK, use Lancashire or feta instead of Cojita, and mozzarella instead of Oaxacan cheese.

NOPALES
The pads of the Opuntia cactus, prickly pear. I haven't included any recipes for nopales because fresh ones are hard to get here and tinned ones are not good in the salads Mexicans make with them.

TOMATILLOS
See above – fresh tomatillos are great if you can get them (see suppliers page 308).

TORTILLAS

A tortilla is a flat disc of cooked corn or flour dough. You can make your own tortillas (pages 43 and 44) or buy them. Corn tortillas will need to be ordered from specialist shops or online. I advise buying the larger packs and freezing them in small quantities well sealed in sandwich bags, ready to pull out when you need them. The following list explains all the different names and variations.

BURRITO
Usually a large flour tortilla, generously stuffed with meat, fish, beans, cheese, cooked rice, guacamole and salsas in any combination, then rolled with the ends tucked in to contain the fillings.

ENCHILADA
Literally means 'in chilli' – a stuffed and folded or rolled tortilla covered in salsa (red or green) and usually topped with grated or crumbled cheese, soured cream and coriander.

FAJITAS
Tex-Mex name for any grilled meat in a taco with salsas.

FLAUTA
A filled tortilla that's rolled like a flute.

HUARACHE
A large oval tortilla shaped like a huarache sandal.

NACHOS
Tex-Mex dish of fried tortillas with salsas and usually cheese.

PANUCHO
A refried stuffed tortilla from the Yucatán.

QUESADILLA
A fried tortilla (corn or flour) stuffed with cheese.

TACO
A filled tortilla.

TLAYUDA
A large open-faced tortilla – ie, not folded.

TOSTADA
A tortilla that's been deep fried or baked until crisp.

TOTOPO
A fried or baked segment of a tortilla.

WARMING TORTILLAS
You can warm tortillas in a dry frying pan, in a microwave or in the oven. Don't overdo it, you want them to be soft and pliable not crisp – 30 seconds on each side in a pan, 30 seconds for up to five tortillas in the microwave, and 7 minutes for up to five in a medium (180°C/Fan 160°C) oven is about right. It's a good idea to brush a little water over the tortillas if they are more than a day old.

Keep the tortillas warm in foil, on a plate covered with foil, or in a tortilla basket with a lid (a *tortillero*), which you certainly will have bought home if you've holidayed in Mexico. Or you can buy an insulated fabric pouch, adorned with a Day of the Dead skull, on the Internet for about £8.00.

COOK'S TIPS

I like my recipes to be as easy to use as possible. Generally, I don't specify the weight of garlic cloves, tomatoes, carrots or onions because the reality of cooking is you just take a clove or two of garlic or a whole onion or a few turns of the peppermill. However, I thought it would be sensible to suggest the weights (unpeeled) that I have in mind:

1 garlic clove: 5g
1 small onion: 100g
1 medium onion: 175g
1 large onion: 225g
10 turns peppermill: about ⅛ tsp
20 turns peppermill: about ¼ tsp
Small handful fresh herbs: about 15g
Large handful fresh herbs: about 30g

All teaspoon and tablespoon measurements are level unless otherwise stated and are based on measuring spoons:

1 teaspoon = 5ml
1 tablespoon = 15ml

Readers in Australia need to make minor adjustments, as their tablespoon measure is 20ml.

OVEN TEMPERATURES

We have given settings for regular and fan ovens throughout the book. Should you need gas settings, they are as follows:

°C	°C FAN	GAS
120	100	½
140	120	1
150	130	2
160	140	3
180	160	4
190	170	5
200	180	6
220	200	7
230	210	8
240	220	9

AVOCADOS

The best way to remove an avocado stone is first to put the avocado on a chopping board and cut it all the way around. Twist the two halves to separate them. Lay the half with the stone uppermost on the board. Lightly chop into the stone to embed the part of the knife near the heel in the stone, then twist the knife to remove the stone from the avocado. Scoop the flesh from the skin with a large spoon. To remove the stone from the knife, knock the stone on the edge of a chopping board. Always sprinkle avocados with lime or lemon juice if not eating immediately, as the flesh turns brown once exposed to the air. To ripen hard avocados more quickly, put them in a brown paper bag.

BUTTERFLYING FISH

Plan A: Ask the fishmonger to gut, scale and butterfly the fish.

Plan B: Trim the fins and cut from the anus at the back of the belly cavity, opening the fish up down to the tail. Either remove the head or snip out the gills and open it up by cutting through under the head. Spread the fish belly-side down on a chopping board and press firmly along the backbone until the fish is completely flat. Remove the backbone by snipping through it at the head and just before the tail and gently pulling it out.

DEVEINING PRAWNS

To remove the intestinal tract from prawns (known as deveining), you need a small sharp knife. Run the knife down two-thirds of the length of the prawn shell from the back of the head towards the tail. Using the tip of the knife, hook out the dark-coloured thread – it usually comes out in one piece – and discard it.

USEFUL EQUIPMENT

COMAL

A heavy cast-iron pan, for cooking tortillas and charring chillies, but you can use any shallow pan with a non-stick coating.

FOOD THERMOMETER

To take the guesswork out of cooking temperatures.

MOLCAJETE

A heavy stone pestle and mortar.

TORTILLA PRESS

If you decide to invest in a tortilla press I suggest getting an aluminum one; the steel ones tend to break if dropped. You will need to use a sheet of something like cling film top and bottom to stop the dough sticking or a plastic sandwich bag works perfectly – just cut it into two sheets.

SUPPLIERS

The following carry stocks of chillies, Mexican flour, sauces and other storecupboard items, plus some fresh produce.

AMAZON
www.amazon.co.uk

COOL CHILE COMPANY
www.coolchile.co.uk
0208 969 5640

LA TIENDITA
www.latiendita.co.uk
0207 736 0897
Many thanks for supplying the chillies for the photograph on pages 12–13

MEXICAN GROCER
www.mexgrocer.co.uk
01582 391511

SOUTH DEVON CHILLI FARM
www.southdevonchillifarm.co.uk
01548 550782

INDEX

ACKNOWLEDGEMENTS

Thanks to the following at Ebury Books – Rebecca Smart, Managing Director, Lizzy Gray, Publishing Director, Charlotte Macdonald, Editor, and my publicist Claire Scott. Fulsome praise to my copy editor Jinny Johnson who has always been at the end of the telephone.

Enormous thanks to Portia Spooner who has collated and tested the recipes. She also went to Mexico for a long research trip with Arezoo Farhazad from Denham Productions which made for successful comparing of notes when writing the book. Thanks to Arezoo for her knowledge of Mexican cuisine and expert pronunciation!

For their vital role in making *The Road to Mexico* look so lovely, thanks to Alex and Emma Smith who designed the book, and James Murphy, who took every one of the beautiful photographs and with whom I've now been working for 18 years. Also thanks to Aya Nishimura for her beautiful food styling and Penny Markham for so expertly matching the pots, plates and pans to the food photography from so many New World cities. Thanks to Andy Smith for his fabulous illustrations.

For *The Road to Mexico* TV programme, thanks to David Pritchard, Producer and Director, and Ben Southwell who directed out in California and Mexico. Thanks, too, to cameraman Chris Topliss and sound recordist Pete Underwood, not forgetting a few occasional helpers – Lucy Musca for testing recipes and Luis Reyes and Lexis-Olivier Ray, second cameramen and drone operators in Mexico and California, and Verity Oswin, Cath Cuevas and Maritza Carbajal who were such perfect local fixers in Mexico.

I'd also like to thank Grace Kitto, researchers Liz Stone and Adrienne Doyard and the rest of the tireless team at Denhams without whom the TV series would not happen.

A big thank you to Viv Taylor and Jane Rees for coordinating everything in Padstow. Finally, to my wife Sas who wanted so much to come to Mexico because she loves it so mu but couldn't because of Olive's GCSEs but nevertheless, as always, was tireless in her supp particularly in trying so many Mexican dishes.